ENQUIRING MINDS

Socratic Dialogue in Education

ENQUIRING MINDS
Socratic Dialogue in Education

Edited by
Rene Saran and Barbara Neisser

Society for the Furtherance of the
Critical Philosophy (UK)

Philosophical-Political Academy (Germany)

Trentham Books
Stoke on Trent, UK and Sterling, USA

Trentham Books Limited

Westview House	22883 Quicksilver Drive
734 London Road	Sterling
Oakhill	VA 20166-2012
Stoke on Trent	USA
Staffordshire	
England ST4 5NP	

© 2004 Rene Saran and Barbara Neisser

All rights reserved. No part of this publication may be reproduced or transmitted in any form or by any means, electronic or mechanical including photocopying, recording or any information storage or retrieval system, without prior permission in writing from the publishers.

First published 2004, reprinted 2006

British Library Cataloguing-in-Publication Data
A catalogue record for this book is available from the British Library

ISBN-13: 978-1-85856-336-7
ISBN-10: 1-85856-336-4

Designed and typeset by Trentham Print Design Ltd., Chester.

Contents

Foreword • vii
Tamsyn Imison
Preface and acknowledgements • ix
The Contributors • xi

PART I
The Socratic Method and education

Chapter 1
Introduction • 1
Rene Saran and Barbara Neisser

Chapter 2
Socratic Dialogue and self-directed learning • 9
Dieter Birnbacher and Dieter Krohn

Chapter 3
Theory and practice of Socratic Dialogue • 15
Dieter Krohn

PART II
Experience in schools

Chapter 4
The challenge of Socratic Dialogue in education • 25
Tamsyn Imison

Chapter 5
Socratic Dialogue in teaching ethics and philosophy: organisational issues • 29
Rene Saran and Barbara Neisser

Chapter 6
Experiences with Socratic Dialogue in primary schools • 41
Ingrid Delgehausen

Chapter 7
Socratic Dialogue – my first experience • 47
Rene Saran

Chapter 8
**Experiences with Socratic Dialogue
in secondary schools** • 53
Rene Saran

Chapter 9
**'We had to think for ourselves' – using Socratic Dialogue in
mathematics lessons in a secondary school** • 71
Mechthild Goldstein

Chapter 10
**Socratic Dialogue in philosophy teaching
in the sixth form** • 79
Barbara Neisser

PART III
Theory in relation to practice

Chapter 11
The Socratic approach at school level: four models • 93
Gisela Raupach-Strey

Chapter 12
Six pedagogical measures and Socratic facilitation • 107
Gustav Heckmann

Chapter 13
The Socratic Method • 121
Leonard Nelson
– with an introduction by *Fernando Leal*

Further Information

Appendix 1
Organisations offering Socratic activities • 167

Appendix 2
Socratic Dialogue – procedures and rules • 171

Appendix 3
Literature survey on Socratic Dialogue by Fernando Leal • 175

Appendix 4
Original sources – the editors acknowledgement of
permissions and citing of original sources • 181

Foreword

As Chair of the UK Society for the Furtherance of the Critical Philosophy (SFCP), it gives me the greatest pleasure to invite you to use and enjoy this important book *Enquiring Minds – Socratic Dialogue in Education*. The SFCP and our German based sister organisation, the Philosophical-Political Academy (PPA), are both registered charities and are sponsoring this publication by Trentham Books.

The co-editors Rene Saran, a Trustee and Secretary of SFCP and Barbara Neisser, a Trustee and Vice-Chair of PPA, practise what they preach and this challenging task has been accomplished not only with rigour but also with humour and consensus to an exacting schedule. Many others who are important in this area have also contributed.

Interest in the Socratic Dialogue is growing amongst educators and this publication is timely, with all schools and colleges wishing to develop meaningful activities that may 'grow' the 'good' citizens of the future. Most schools and colleges now have councils or other democratic forums where participants will need training in dialogue.

Both our Societies have been participating in Socratic Dialogues for many years and we are now actively encouraging all educators to add Socratic Dialogue to their armoury of effective practice.

This book is an essential tool for everyone working in education, both those training others in the use of Socratic Dialogue and those who wish to be trained in order to use it to support all learning and enquiry. It will also develop the reflective and ethical approaches of both young people and adults, by encouraging the building of consensus instead of combative debate.

Tamsyn Imison
Chair SFCP
Former Headteacher of Hampstead School –
a London inner city comprehensive
January 2004

Preface and acknowledgements

The editors of this book, Rene Saran and Barbara Neisser, met and became friends many years ago through their Socratic work and their shared interest in educational problems and developments. Their deepening friendship grew around these common interests and laid the basis for various projects in Socratic philosophy.

In 2002, an International Conference on Socratic Dialogue and Civil Society took place in Birmingham, UK. It was planned by the Society for the Furtherance of the Critical Philosophy (SFCP) and the German organisations Philosophical-Political Academy (PPA) and Society of Socratic Facilitators (GSP), with support from the Dutch Network of Socratics. Some hundred people from twenty countries in Europe and beyond, many from countries where English is spoken as the first foreign language, took part. Direct personal communication across the nationalities encouraged reflection about ethical values and attitudes with reference to the process of globalisation.

During the conference they experienced Socratic Dialogue groups which they appreciated as a valuable form of communication. Workshops dealt with problems experienced in civil society in Eastern and Western Europe as well as in other parts of the world. Many participants were particularly impressed by the potential of Socratic Dialogue in fostering intercultural understanding. Again and again they asked for literature in English to further and deepen their interest in this topic.

Teachers in schools and higher education were looking for descriptions of Socratic experience and for practical guidance for conducting Socratic Dialogues. But most of the relevant available texts were published only in German. Recognising the need for English language texts, the editors conceived the idea of this volume which would include translations of the most important theoretical and practical texts on Socratic Dialogue, and the available articles in English on this topic.

The editors wish to thank all the German and English authors who agreed to make their previously published work available and who gave support in the translation of their texts. Special thanks are due to Paul Penny for preparing the final manuscript; to Sue Hogg for scanning some texts and converting them into word documents; to Dorothy Moir and Keith Hammond for commenting on and correcting some of the texts.

The editors also wish to thank Fernando Leal for his advice on and careful corrections to the manuscript, and for the updating of the previously published overview of the most important literature about the Socratic Method. Thanks also to Dieter Krohn for his support and for securing the agreement of copyright holders of the German texts.

Finally, thanks are due to the SFCP and the PPA for covering the cost of translations and certain other essential expenditure.

The editors hope that the book will have many interested readers, that the international Socratic network will be strengthened and that European cooperation between people undertaking Socratic work will be enhanced and strengthened.

Rene Saran, London, UK
Barbara Neisser, Cologne, Germany
January 2004

The contributors

Chapter 2 **Dieter Birnbacher**
PhD (1973) after studies in philosophy, English and linguistics at the Universities of Düsseldorf, Cambridge and Hamburg; Habilitation University of Essen (1988); Professor of Philosophy, University of Düsseldorf (1996-present) and University of Dortmund (1993-1996). Main fields of interest: ethics, applied ethics, anthropology. Main publications: *Die Logik der Kriterien. Analysen zur Spätphilosophie Wittgensteins* (1974) [*The logic of criteria: studies on Wittgenstein's later philosophy*]; *Verantwortung für zukünftige Generationen* (1988) [*Responsibility for future generations*]; *Tun und Unterlassen* (1995) [*Action and Omission*]; *Analytische Einführung in die Ethik* (2003) [*Analytical introduction to ethics*]. Vice-President of Schopenhauer-Gesellschaft; Member of several permanent commissions of the German Medical Association (Bundesärztekammer); Member of Philosophical-Political Academy (PPA).

Chapters 2, 3 **Dieter Krohn**
PhD (1980); Moderator for English as a foreign language in comprehensive schools in Lower Saxony (1991-present); former Comprehensive School Teacher; Executive Member of Philosophical-Political Academy (PPA); Chair of German Society of Socratic Facilitators (GSP); numerous publications in German about Socratic Dialogue and on teaching English as a foreign language.

Chapter 4 **Tamsyn Imison**
Deputy Head then Headteacher of London Comprehensive Schools (retired from Hampstead School 2000); Member of numerous Committees and on Executive of Secondary Heads Association (SHA); freelance Consultant (since retirement); Chair of Society for the Furtherance of the Critical Philosophy (SFCP).

Chapters 1, 5, 7, 8 **Rene Saran** *(Co-editor)*
PhD (1968) 'Secondary Schools Policy and Administration'; Senior, then Principal Lecturer, City of London Polytechnic, now Guildhall University (retired 1986); extensive research on education policy and management; thirty years as school governor of primary and secondary schools in London; worked in industry and commerce and as Editorial Assistant on *Socialist Commentary*; Secretary of Society for the Furtherance of the Critical Philosophy (SFCP); Member of Philosophical-Political Academy (PPA) and German Society of Socratic Facilitators (GSP); Hon Vice-President of British Educational, Leadership, Management and Administration Society (BELMAS); sole and joint author/editor of several books and articles; Socratic facilitator in schools and in adult education.

Chapters 1, 5, 10 **Barbara Neisser** *(Co-editor)*
Subject director of student teacher training in Cologne (1997-present); teacher at Comprehensive School in Cologne (1987-1996); Research Assistant in philosophy, University of Saarbrücken (1981-1986); Vice-Chair of Philosophical-Political Academy (PPA); Socratic facilitator in schools and adult education; Member of German Society of Socratic Facilitators (GSP); author of articles on Socratic Method, teamwork, conflict resolution in school, and sixth form development; co-editor of German series on Socratic philosophising.

Chapter 6 **Ingrid Delgehausen**
Headteacher of primary school near Hannover (1998-present); class teacher in different types of schools in Lower Saxony (1973-1998); facilitator of Socratic Dialogues in school and in adult education; Member of German Society of Socratic Facilitators (GSP).

Chapter 9 **Mechthild Goldstein**
Teacher of mathematics and philosophy in secondary modern school in Paderborn (1996-present); facilitator of Socratic Dialogues in school and in adult education, primarily in mathematical topics; Member of German Society of Socratic Facilitators (GSP); initiated that Society's group network on internet.

THE CONTRIBUTORS

Chapter 11 **Gisela Raupach-Strey**
PhD *Sokratische Didaktik* (2002) [*Socratic Teaching*]; Research Assistant in the pedagogy of the philosophy and ethics curriculum, University of Halle (1998-present); Grammar School teacher in philosophy and mathematics in Hannover (1984-1998); author of school texts and of many articles on curriculum and on Socratic Dialogue; Socratic facilitator; Member of Philosophical-Political Academy (PPA) and German Society of Socratic Facilitators (GSP).

Chapter 12 **Gustav Heckmann** (1898-1996)
PhD (1924, in physics); worked in adult education in the school founded by Leonard Nelson in pre-war Germany; refugee during Nazi-era; Professor of Philosophy and Education, University of Hannover (1946-1982); organised Socratic seminars both at the University of Hannover and for the Philosophical-Political Academy (PPA); trained Socratic facilitators; author of *Das Sokratische Gespräch* [*Socratic Dialogue*] (1981, 2nd ed 1993); Member of PPA.

Chapter 13 **Leonard Nelson** (1882-1927)
Professor of Philosophy, University of Göttingen; founder in 1922 of an experimental school for children and of a college for adults (using the Socratic Method as a key approach to learning); founder of Philosophical-Political Academy (PPA, 1922); author of collected works on philosophy, epistemology, law and government, politics, ethics and education (nine volumes).

Chapter 13, Appendix 3 **Fernando Leal**
PhD (1983) *Der aristotelische Wahrheitsbegriff und die Aufgabe der Semantik* [*The Aristotelian concept of truth and the task of semantics*]; Professor of Social Science, University of Guadalajara, Mexico (1993-present); founded Linguistics Institute for the Study of Indian Languages, University of Guadalajara; long-standing interest in Critical Philosophy; author of numerous articles and contributions to books; participant and facilitator of Socratic Dialogues; Honorary Research Fellow, Society for the Furtherance of the Critical Philosophy (SFCP).

PART I
The Socratic Method and education

1
INTRODUCTION

Rene Saran and Barbara Neisser

In his seminal piece, 'What is Enlightenment?' Kant stated that the motto of that remarkable period in European thought was quite simply 'Have courage to use your own understanding'. Kant provided the framework within which Leonard Nelson later developed his educational philosophy in the 1920s. Nelson made the concept of thinking for oneself, or self-directed learning, central to his philosophy of education. For the learner this involved the growth of individual autonomy in the development of the capacity to reason.

Nelson saw the Socratic Method as especially suited for fostering the capacities of enquiry and reason. The method consists of a learning-teaching process in which learners, through co-operative group dialogue, win knowledge about their own inner experience and develop insights into the truth concerning a philosophical question. In this process they are guided by a facilitator who steers the dialogue without impinging on the substance of the self-directed enquiry of the learners (see chapter 13 for Nelson's essay The Socratic Method).

By following the dialogical procedures recorded by Plato in the early dialogues of Socrates, Socratic Dialogue enables ordinary people to philosophise with the aim of enriching and informing civic life. This involves a non-specialist way of philosophising that has been furthered through the neo-Kantian philosophical practices of Nelson, Heckmann and, more recently, a number of other philosophers.

Gustav Heckmann, a student of Nelson, developed these ideas further and introduced the Socratic Method, evolved into a teaching-learning dialogue, into his work as a teacher-trainer in post-war Germany. His chief concern was that teachers of the future should develop into independent personalities and become competent to foster self-directed learning, as well as developing the capacity to elicit reasoned judgements among children, young people and adults.

Stimulated by the work of Gustav Heckmann, a tradition of Socratic Dialogue developed in Germany and the Netherlands, and resulted in many publications. Nowadays, there exists a widely spread practice of Socratic Dialogue in schools and adult education (*see* appendix 1 for organisations offering Socratic activities and appendix 3 for survey of the literature).

Theory and practice are often separated in the concerns of school and academia. But when theory and practice relate to the knowledge of non-academic everyday life issues, they become less easy to separate – for instance, the way people reason about life invariably informs their everyday conduct.

In his teaching Leonard Nelson sought unity between theory and practice. In 1922, he established a boarding school for children (the *Walkemühle*) and an academy for adult education (the Philosophical-Political Academy – PPA) in order to test his educational concepts in real life situations. Teachers in the school and in the academy used the Socratic Method in their professional work.

After 1933, both school and PPA were banned under the Nazi regime. It is noteworthy that many who had attended Nelson's Academy and joined the political movement founded by him became active underground anti-fascists in opposition to Hitler. Susanne Miller, a German historian, has written about the importance of participation in Socratic Dialogues during those dark times. It was this participation that sustained those who took part in the underground resistance, enabling them to retain and deepen their inner convictions in the fight for survival under Nazi tyranny. In 1949 the PPA, but not the school for children, was re-established in Germany.

THE SOCRATIC METHOD AND EDUCATION

Socratic Dialogue encourages ordinary human reflection in a dialogue setting. At times, and in certain settings, such a dialogue can be extremely powerful for people of all backgrounds. What is special about Socratic Dialogue is that it is open to all who wish to engage in a co-operative thinking activity where the basic aims are:

- To answer a philosophical question by seeking out the truth about the nature of concepts like tolerance, freedom, justice and responsibility, and to endeavour to reach consensus – ie to reach a result or *outcome*

- To engage in the co-operative activity of seeking answers to questions and to understand each other through the exploration of *concrete experiences*, volunteered by participants, one of which is usually chosen by the group for detailed analysis. In this way all are engaged in the *process*

- To deepen individual *insights and understandings* as the dialogic process moves towards enabling participants to grasp the moral perplexities of the everyday world

- To gain through dialogue greater clarity about what is and what is not in keeping with considered, thoughtful and reasonable conduct, thus enhancing self-confidence in our ability to reason and so shaping our *approach to life*

Participants may not reach definitive *outcomes* in the form of agreed answers. This need not lead to disappointment. The positive experience of participation in co-operative thinking is of major importance; it can be very rewarding as a *learning process* and have *profound meaning for one's life*. The process of Socratic Dialogue is governed by a set of rules. These are frequently elaborated and applied in many of the chapters of this book. A summary of these rules is provided in appendix 2.

In today's educational practice, questions are raised about the methods available to help learners to develop skills in self-directed activity and philosophical reflection. Most would agree that it is important that schools should focus on independent learning and intellectual activity. In the information age, in which the electronic media (videos, computers, electronic games) can place children and young people in passive learning situations, intellectual and communicative potential is often inadequately supported and developed, especially during the formative years of childhood and adolescence.

Contemporary educational theory embraces a concept of learning which is similar to the self-directed learning of Socratic Dialogue in that it involves enquiry into inner activity and the independent development of cognitive and emotional competences.

Central to Socratic philosophy is the moral agent, the human agent who has to think about how he or she is to live well with others in social harmony. Reflection on such a problem gains expression in speech. Genuine conversation demands a real willingness to work towards truth with others who are pursuing the same aim. Arrogance, conceit and hostility threaten both social harmony and good dialogue. They jeopardise the philosophical progress that is sought in Socratic Dialogue as the views of one person are tested against the views of others and as more general views about life emerge from different perspectives. The ultimate test is the way these views throw light on the question at hand and consolidate the details of the original example. The reasoning of Socratic Dialogue is thus always anchored in the to and fro movement of the reasoning process, based upon the example given at the start of the dialogue.

Through this kind of thoughtful engagement individuals can learn about life and reflect upon their own experiences. They can develop the capacity to systematically test their own and other people's general judgements, including various views of the world and different political ideologies and theories. The Socratic Method thus offers a process of dialogue through which individuals can gain insight into their spiritual and intellectual outlook and develop their capacity for reasonable argument and their ability to empathise.

The texts in this book illuminate the Socratic Method and introduce readers to the practice of Socratic Dialogue. Many of the chapters that follow are extracts from sources which have been translated from German. Some of these are pedagogical and philosophical scientific contributions to the German literature. During translation some texts have been cut and most footnotes have been omitted as these refer almost exclusively to German literature. The original sources of these texts are given in appendix 4.

THE SOCRATIC METHOD AND EDUCATION

Part I of this book contains texts on the significance of the Socratic Method for learning and on some of its structural characteristics.

Chapter 2 serves as a contemporary introduction to the value of Socratic Dialogue in today's learning environment, in which far more emphasis than hitherto is laid on self-directed independent learning. It is taken from a German text, published in 2002, which collated various theoretical writings published over several decades, thus reflecting the history of modern Socratic Dialogue. It illustrates the link between the Twentieth Century Nelson-Heckmann tradition of Socratic Dialogue and the Socrates of antiquity.

Heckmann's book on *Socratic Dialogue*, originally published in 1981, sets out the basic principles that underpinned his practice as a Socratic facilitator. The editors have selected two chapters from Heckmann's book which focus on key features of facilitation (chapter 12). In the translated text he refers to selected examples to illustrate six pedagogical measures that were central in his practice. All the other contributions in this volume are anchored in these six measures, along with Heckmann's guidance for Socratic facilitators on how to steer the dialogue. These measures are the base for the practice of all facilitators in Germany, Britain and the Netherlands.

In chapter 3 Dieter Krohn, a student of Heckmann, gives an invaluable overview of the history and philosophical foundations of Socratic Dialogue in the Twentieth Century. In addition, he provides an informative summary of the indispensable characteristics of contemporary Socratic practice.

Part II describes Socratic Dialogue experiences in different types of schools in England and Germany.

In chapter 4 Tamsyn Imison provides the bridge between the more theoretical contributions to this volume and the more practical and applied chapters. A great believer in 'the ethical school', she suggests that use of the Socratic Method in schools can have direct relevance to the development of ethical awareness among both students and staff. During her sixteen years as headteacher of a large and successful comprehensive secondary school in London, she was able to introduce Socratic Dialogue to her students. Rene Saran, who facilitated these dialogues, reports on them in part II.

The material in chapter 5 was first produced as a joint workshop at an international conference held in Germany. It focuses on ethics lessons in England and Germany, and the organisational and practical conditions appropriate for successful Socratic Dialogues in particular settings. Different stages of the dialogue, the meta-dialogue and the changed role of the teacher are explained. The legal framework within which the Socratic approach can be introduced in these two countries is described.

Chapter 6 moves to the primary sector. Ingrid Delgehausen, also one of Heckmann's students, has experimented with the use of Socratic Dialogue in a German village primary school with children aged seven to nine. She demonstrates the capacity of young children to deal systematically and intensively with philosophical questions. Delgehausen's chapter illustrates the use of Raupach-Strey's Model 2, set out in chapter 11.

Chapters 7 and 8 contain Rene Saran's reports on her early endeavours to introduce Socratic Dialogue in some secondary comprehensive schools in England. Chapter 6 has appeared previously in both Britain and Germany. Chapter 7 gives an account of experiences at a number of schools, often with mixed age groups, when it proved important to address questions that were directly relevant to school life. This engaged the active interest of the students and promoted their creative thinking about possible solutions to down-to-earth daily concerns, vividly portrayed in their examples. The young people's own evaluation of their Socratic Dialogue experience is included in these reports.

In chapter 9 Mechthild Goldstein describes the use of the Socratic Method in the teaching of mathematics. She shows how fourteen to fifteen year old students in a German secondary modern school worked on and solved, by their own efforts, a geometrical problem. They were proud of their achievement, saying that 'we had to think for ourselves'. Both Nelson and Heckmann had emphasised the importance of Socratic Dialogue for mathematical logical thinking and for the teaching of mathematics. Goldstein studied with Heckmann's student Hartmut Spiegel, who, with Rainer Loska, extended the use of Socratic Dialogue in the teaching of mathematics by developing models for primary and secondary schools.

Barbara Neisser describes, in chapter 10, one of her experiences with Socratic Dialogue in sixth form philosophy lessons in Germany. She shows how a complete Socratic Dialogue can be organised and conducted within the framework of the school, and describes the process of the dialogue and its results. This contribution concludes with an evaluation on the teaching-learning process and illustrates Raupach-Strey's Model 1 in practice (chapter 11).

Thus Part II offers practical examples of how critical thinking and communication skills are fostered in Socratic Dialogue sessions in schools. Thoughtful young people are often searching for ways to shape their lives in the community. Personal and social relations loom large. Alongside their keen interest in the wider issues of the world, they feel the need to resolve, in a considerate and reasonable manner, the many practical and everyday challenges which face them. Such young people have much to gain from being introduced to the Socratic Method.

Part III includes some basic and historical texts about the Socratic Method. In chapter 11, Gisela Raupach-Strey presents four models that form part of a more extensive work in German about Socratic pedagogy. The four models point to ways in which Socratic Dialogue and elements of Socratic Dialogue can be integrated into the process of learning and teaching in school. Raupach-Strey's strategic and organisational suggestions might well be transferable to other educational settings.

Reference has been made above to Heckmann's work *Socratic Dialogue*, on which the editors have drawn for chapter 12. In chapter 13, the 1922 essay by Leonard Nelson on the Socratic Method is reproduced, with an introduction by Fernando Leal. This is an essential foundation text in the history of the Socratic Method. In this essay, Nelson presented his concept of Socratic Dialogue that laid the basis for all further Twentieth Century development.

Recommended further reading

Birnbacher, Dieter (1999) The Socratic Method in teaching medical ethics: potential and limitations, *Medicine, Health Care and Philosophy*, 2, pp219-224

Boele, Dries (1997) The 'Benefits' of a Socratic Dialogue, or: Which results can we promise? *Inquiry: Critical Thinking Across the Disciplines*, XVII(3), pp48-70

Bolten, Hans (2001) Managers develop Moral Accountability: the impact of Socratic Dialogue, Reason in Practice, *The Journal of Philosophy of Management*, 1(3), pp21-34

Heckmann, Gustav (1987) Socratic Dialogue, *Thinking, The Journal of Philosophy for Children*, 8(1), pp34-37

Henry-Hermann, Grete (1991) Conquering Chance, *Philosophical Investigations*, 14 (1), pp1-80

Kessels, Jos and Korthagen, Fred A J (1997) The relationship between theory and practice: back to the classics, *Educational Researcher*, 25(3), pp17-22

Kessels, Jos (2001) Socrates comes to Market. Reason in Practice, *The Journal of Philosophy of Management*, 1(1), pp49-71

Kessels, Jos (2002) Schooling and Free Space, available at http://www.hotniewetrivium.nl/uk/publications/index.html

Leal, Fernando and Saran, Rene (2000) A Dialogue on the Socratic Dialogue, *Occasional Working Papers in Ethics and Critical Philosophy*, ed Shipley, Patricia, 2, pp51-57, London, SFCP

Leal, Fernando and Saran, Rene (2004, forthcoming) A Dialogue on the Socratic Dialogue, Act Two, *op cit*, 3, London, SFCP

Loska, Rainer (1997) Teaching without instruction, the Neo-Socratic Method, Paper given at International Congress of Mathematics Education, Quebec, Canada

Miller, Susie (2000) Critical Philosophy as a demand for resistance against National Socialism, *Occasional Working Papers in Ethics and Critical Philosophy*, ed Shipley, Patricia, 2, pp5-12, London, SFCP

Nelson, Leonard (1949) *Socratic Method and Critical Philosophy*, trans. by Brown III, Thomas K, Introduction by Kraft, Julius, New Haven, Yale University Press (this is the source in which Nelson's essay of 1922 on The Socratic Method first appeared in English. It is reproduced as Chapter 13 in this volume)

2
SOCRATIC DIALOGUE AND SELF-DIRECTED LEARNING

Dieter Birnbacher and Dieter Krohn

This text is the introduction to a German book entitled *Socratic Dialogue*, published in 2002, edited by Dieter Birnbacher and Dieter Krohn. The volume is a collection of articles on the theory and essays about Socratic Dialogue spanning several decades from 1922 to 1999. The link between the Nelson – Heckmann tradition of Socratic Dialogue and the Socrates of antiquity is illuminated. The significance and structure of contemporary Socratic Dialogue are portrayed in relation to their importance for learning processes. Several texts from *Socratic Dialogue* are included in this volume (chapters 10, 12 and 13).

The Socratic or maieutic method has long been an established part of self-directed learning. Its basic idea is to guide the student towards an independent analysis of philosophical or mathematical problems and towards the development of ways of solving them without directly pointing out the solution, or the paths towards it. Maieutics means the skill of the midwife: the teacher is the midwife supporting the student's own efforts to illuminate the truth.

If this method is called 'Socratic' it is not because Socrates, as he appears to us in Plato's dialogues, could be regarded as the model of the Socratic teacher. The figure of Socrates, as we find it in Plato, realises the idea of the Socratic teacher only very inadequately. Over extensive passages he leads his dialogue partner, even manipulates them, and does not always leave the learner the freedom to find the solution to his task by his own effort. If the Socratic Method nevertheless reminds us of Socrates, then it is because it proceeds from similar didactic and epistemological premises: what matters is to allow the dialogue partner to discover the truth for himself or herself; that truth is equally accessible to any reasonable person of good will. Furthermore, finding the truth requires not only the courage to use one's own intellect but also – since truth often lies hidden behind a veil of conventions, prejudice and illusions – a certain deliberate effort of the will to overcome mental laziness and conformity.

The method of the Socratic Dialogue is an extension and development of the Socratic Method, essentially dating back to the Göttingen philosopher and pedagogue Leonard Nelson (1882-1927) and his disciple Gustav Heckmann (1898-1996). These philosophers shared a marked interest in mathematics, as well as an overt engagement in socialist politics. Nelson's idea of developing the Socratic Method into a methodology of group dialogue is closely linked, on the one hand, to his acceptance of the philosophy of Jakob Friedrich Fries (1773-1843), which interpreted the Kantian *a priori* as a kind of psychological given fact. On the other hand, Nelson, as a political leader, felt the need to structure rationally the training of political activists. In contrast to the stringent Socratic Dialogue, which is always strictly limited to two partners, as we find it in Plato, the Nelsonian Socratic Dialogue is a conversation in a group. Each participant has the opportunity to act as 'midwife' for the development of the ideas of every other participant. Ideally this leads not to the insight of a single individual, but to philosophical or mathematical knowledge that is shared by all members of the group.

The change from dialogue between two individuals to dialogue in a group fundamentally transforms the role of the Socratic teacher. He is relieved of some of his maieutic tasks, as every participant is now available as a midwife for every other. At the same time, however, his tasks are extended as a result of the greater complexity of group interaction and the much greater danger that in its quest for truth the group might digress from the path of sequential logical thought or lose sight of the original question.

Heckmann's contribution to the development of the method of Socratic Dialogue consists, among other things, of his detaching the method from the specific neo-Kantian background assumptions with which Nelson linked it, and providing Socratic Dialogue with a broader basis. According to Nelson, philosophical truth is attainable by asking questions about the presuppositions of our everyday changing thought-patterns. The method of 'regression', of systematic search for the most universal foundations of our view of the world and of ourselves – along with the method of 'deduction' – should lead to a series of transcendental truths of universal and absolute validity. Like his models Kant and Fries, Nelson proceeded from the existence of objectively valid philosophical truths, both in theoretical and in practical philosophy. What Nelson – adopting one of Fries's concepts – called the 'self-confidence of reason' is nothing less than the claim that human reflection is capable of discovering such universal truths.

With Heckmann, the method of Socratic Dialogue acquires a more independent role. Nelson's idea that the consensus reached in a group dialogue can be identified with 'the truth' is weakened. Even though truth as a regulative idea continues to be indispensable, a group consensus that has been reached can by no means be regarded as an infallible criterion of truth. Beyond this, learning targets related to Socratic procedures, such as the development of argumentative competence, take their place alongside the aim to comprehend knowledge. The latter is governed by the Kantian ideals of rationality, clarity, autonomy and authenticity. Each participant should say what they really think; they should not maintain any theses merely for strategic reasons or for the sake of mere disputation. Also preserved is the method of *regressive abstraction* that goes back to Fries.

This method, similar to the inductive method, proceeds from the particular in order to arrive at the general, even though generalisation about empirical cases is excluded. Rather, it should be shown that the general is contained in the particular and developed from an analysis of the particular. The starting point for processes of regressive thought are thus not textbook problems but concrete questions against the background of personal experience. Reflective thinking should 'gain a foothold in the concrete'. From there it should progress successively to the abstract and the general. Wherever the method is applied – in ethics, in the theory of knowledge, in mathematics or in introspective psychology – the central idea consists of proceeding from concrete experiences or judgements and, from them, striving to reach universally valid statements, rules or principles.

Characteristic of the method of Socratic Dialogue is the relatively strict regulation of facilitator and participant behaviour. The first rule for the Socratic facilitator states that he (*sic*) should exert his authority only in matters of procedure but not in matters of content. His task is to steer the discussion in such a way that the initial question is kept in view, but that simultaneously as many different solutions as possible are explored and tested for their validity. He is not permitted to introduce his own theories or solutions, just as he should refrain from lecturing on other philosophers' approaches to the solution. As moderator of the group dialogue (called 'facilitator' in English) he should remain as neutral as possible, making sure that all participants are given a chance to make their own contributions.

The second important task of the facilitator is to see to clarity and transparency. This does not mean that unclear ideas or incompletely formulated ideas should not be expressed. In that case the group's effort should be directed towards step-by-step clarification of anything that has been said and to test it as to its premises and consequences. Accordingly, the participants are obliged to express themselves as clearly as possible, to endeavour to understand the statements of others and to assist them in the clarification of their own ideas. The third task of the facilitator consists of support for the group in its efforts to reach consensus – not just a superficial but a well-reasoned consensus. As Heckmann expressed it: 'In Socratic Dialogue we wish to get beyond purely subjective opinion. That is why we examine what reasons we have for our assertions and whether these reasons are acknowledged by all as being sufficient'.

In the Socratic Method the principle of gaining a foothold in the concrete is achieved in the dialogue mainly by the participants tabling their own experiences. The facilitator's skill is demonstrated, among other things, by the ability to assess the potential value of the experiences contained in the 'examples' and to choose the right moment when a newly introduced 'example' opens up new and possibly deeper perspectives.

The institution of the *meta-dialogue* has proved successful as a support for Socratic Dialogue (as indeed also for Ruth Cohn's 'theme-centred interaction', a method which in many respects is related to it). Meta-dialogue offers an opportunity to reflect on the course of the dialogue, to comment on the conduct of facilitator and participants and to raise fundamental questions about method and structure of the dialogue. The meta-dialogue also permits agreements to be made that facilitate or promote the course of the actual dialogue. It is of crucial importance that the meta-dialogue is clearly distinguished from the content dialogue and that it does not unduly impinge on the flow of ideas and their connections. As the facilitator's conduct is subject to critical scrutiny in the meta-dialogue, it has become customary that the chairing of the meta-dialogue is assumed by one of the participants.

When Leonard Nelson tested his dialogue method at the school he founded – the Walkemühle near Melsungen (in North Hesse, not far from Kassel) – the suggested topic for the group's dialogue invariably came from the group itself. Nowadays, Socratic seminars are, as a rule, announced with a pre-set question, to avoid prolonged discussion of the topic to be tackled. This nevertheless leaves the group a considerable measure of freedom to decide on the exact interpretation of and approach to the pre-set question. Needless to say, not all questions are suitable for the Socratic Dialogue method. Suitable questions are those which can be discussed without recourse to empirical or historical information that is not available to the group – thus, in particular, *a priori* questions that can be answered by means of 'pure reason'. Moreover, the questions should be sufficiently complex and non-transparent to allow new and productive insights to emerge; and they should be sufficiently interesting to motivate the participants to invest a good deal of continuous and intensive intellectual work.

At present the method of Socratic Dialogue is practised in the most varied contexts – in ethics seminars at universities, in philosophy and ethics lessons in schools, in teacher training, in adult education, in in-service training of leadership personnel and in medical ethics. The method is suitable in all fields where, setting out from a specific problem, general solutions are sought. Socratic Dialogue has proved its value especially outside academic philosophy in that it demands (and promotes) independent reflection by all participants, while simultaneously aiming at mutual cooperation. This means bringing together subjectivity with inter-subjectivity, and individuality with a supra-individual claim to validity. In whatever way the solution is arrived at in a particular Socratic Dialogue, the decisive point is that the solution helps attain insights that go beyond the individual case, claiming universal validity. Only thus does the Socratic form of dialogue remain true to the unmistakably 'Socratic' question about being and essence.

3
THEORY AND PRACTICE OF SOCRATIC DIALOGUE

Dieter Krohn

Dieter Krohn gives a brief overview, drawn from a German book published in 1998, of the historical development and the philosophical foundations of Socratic Dialogue. In addition he provides an informative summary of the important and indispensable characteristics and conditions of contemporary Socratic Dialogue practice.

Introduction

'As a faithful disciple of Socrates and of his great successor Plato, I find it rather difficult to justify my acceptance of your invitation to talk to you about the Socratic Method.' This is how Leonard Nelson began his 1922 lecture to the Pedagogical Society in Göttingen about Socratic Dialogue (chapter 13). He knew well from Plato that philosophising could not be described in words but could only be understood following personal experience and the intensive effort of philosophising oneself. Nelson illustrated his predicament by adding, 'I therefore find myself in a quandary, not unlike that of a violinist who, when asked how he goes about playing the violin, can of course demonstrate his art but cannot explain his technique in abstract terms.'

It is exactly the same nowadays. Socratic Dialogue has been described as a cooperative activity of philosophising, is practised in different institutional settings and has been developed further in both theory and practice. Nevertheless, no one can understand what Socratic Dialogue really means without participating in and experiencing the process several times. Reading this chapter can in no way replace the experience of a Socratic Dialogue. It may, however, arouse interest and re-inforce the willingness to open oneself to the Socratic process of philosophising jointly with others.

In this outline of Socratic Dialogue only the most important aspects can be presented. This is no substitute for the lively discussion found in the extensive literature about its theory and practice.

On hearing the words 'Socratic Dialogue' one initially thinks of the Platonic dialogues. Here, however, the use of these words refers to Socratic Dialogue in the tradition of Leonard Nelson (1882-1927) and Gustav Heckmann (1898-1996). Undoubtedly, this form of philosophising is closely bound up with the name of Socrates. Notwithstanding, it would be a mistake to assume that the Platonic dialogues would convey an appropriate description of Socratic Dialogue as practised today in the Nelson-Heckmann tradition.

Nelson pointedly criticised both the philosophical content and the Socratic facilitation of the Platonic dialogues. By way of example, he drew attention to the lengthy monologues and the use of leading questions. Despite this, Nelson's readiness to describe his own form of philosophising as Socratic rested on his admiration for the basic philosophical and pedagogical attitudes of Socrates. The following criteria were important to Nelson and he formulated them in his speech in a way that may sound somewhat strange to contemporary readers.

> Socrates was the first to combine confidence in the ability of the human mind to recognise philosophical truth [with] the conviction that this truth is not arrived at through occasional bright ideas or mechanical teaching but that only planned, unremitting, and consistent thinking leads us from darkness into its light. Therein lies Socrates' greatness as a philosopher. His greatness as a pedagogue is based on another innovation: he made his pupils do their own thinking and introduced the interchange of ideas as a safeguard against self-deception.

We do not necessarily have to accept Nelson's terminology or his position within the theory of knowledge in order to describe and to uphold our contemporary understanding of Socratic Dialogue.

It will nevertheless be apparent that central elements of Nelson's tradition have been retained. We attempt here to formulate a working definition of Socratic Dialogue, criteria for the selection of possible topics for such dialogues and the rights and responsibilities of the participants in a Socratic Dialogue.

Characteristics and rules of Socratic Dialogue
In a Socratic Dialogue a group of participants with equal rights seek to answer questions or examine statements of a philosophical (or mathematical) nature. In this process the participants, together and systematically, engage in exchange of views, information and reasons aiming at mutual understanding. The purpose of this endeavour is to reach consensus in the group. It is common practice that the group is guided by a facilitator who refrains from intervening in the content but assists in structuring the dialogue and fostering mutual understanding.

What questions is it possible to answer in such a dialogue? What statements can be examined? The questions and statements that are suitable for a Socratic Dialogue are those for which independent critical thinking about personal experience suffices. This includes reflecting on one's own thinking. This means that philosophical and mathematical topics can be tackled, as well as general questions about inner awareness and feeling. Individual psychological problems are excluded since they need to be worked on by means of psychotherapy. Similarly, questions or statements that require expert knowledge are unsuitable. Questions that require information that can only be supplied by empirical research – for example sociological, historical or geographical topics – cannot be answered in a Socratic Dialogue.

A short list of topics, which have been dealt with in various Socratic groups, might serve as further explanation. In some cases the group had to formulate its own question.

- What are the criteria for accepting authority?
- What is quality of life?
- How do we differentiate between true statements and subjective views?
- Speaking and thinking
- Objects of many equal sides, angles and surfaces

- To repeat the same matter in different words
- Are there senseless questions?
- Are we responsible for the future?
- Can reasons be given for an aesthetic judgement?
- What does it mean to act responsibly?

Participants in a Socratic Dialogue have relatively few expectations to fulfil. They have to be willing to express their own thoughts in clear language, make the effort to understand the thoughts of others, and evaluate critically their own contributions and those of others. The views they express must be truly their own and reflect their convictions regarding the truth of the matter. They should not – for the sake of pleasure in debate – defend propositions they do not hold true. In this connection Nelson is concerned with honesty in thinking and speaking. In order to meet these conditions the participants do not need to have knowledge of the views of philosophers. Socratic Dialogue is not history of philosophy but, by contrast, consists of autonomous philosophising.

We cannot take it for granted that a philosophical dialogue will succeed. It might be tiresome and frustrating, full of misunderstandings, without clear structure. It can lose its point or serve people's vanity. Socratic Dialogue tries to avoid these traps by having someone present whose sole responsibility it is to ensure the orderly conduct of the dialogue and mutual understanding. This person is the facilitator. To facilitate a Socratic Dialogue is a very demanding task. It requires deep philosophical insight and sensitivity towards cognitive, emotional and group dynamic processes. Such competences are developed by systematic philosophising, through frequent participation in and gaining experience of facilitating Socratic Dialogues.

In order to allow a better grasp of this type of cooperative philosophising a description of the tasks of Socratic facilitators follows. This might also be interpreted as a description of the Socratic Dialogue rules.

The facilitator has to ensure that real understanding is achieved. As long as the impression remains that a statement is understood differently by participants the dialogue has to focus on this particular statement until full understanding is reached. This is accomplished, for example, by asking group members to repeat how they understood someone else or by asking a particular person whether she or he feels correctly understood.

The facilitator has to ensure that the group remains with its chosen question until it has been sufficiently clarified, as far as this is possible, at a particular stage of development. All present have always to know which question is under discussion at that moment. Whenever the group goes off at a tangent the facilitator has to bring it back to the original question. If the group wishes to conclude its work on a question, because participants think that it is necessary first to answer another question or think that they are making no progress, then the decision has to be a conscious one, based on reasons, taken by the group. One should, however, protect the group from an overly long discussion about the choice of the next question.

The facilitator has to ensure that the dialogue does not end up in empty speculation, but – on the contrary – that participants keep their feet firmly on the ground. They have to be induced to work from the concrete and always to have the concrete in mind when they progress towards general statements. In most cases this is achieved by use of an example based on the personal experience of a group member.

Now and then there are discussions as to whether the facilitator is permitted to take up a position in matters of content. Nelson had an unambiguous view on this question. He held the view that facilitator intervention on matters of content was never admissible because the expression of facilitator judgements would prevent students reaching their own conclusions. Heckmann took a less rigid position. For him the work of the facilitator is to be based on the main aim, which is to assist participants to work out their own insights. This means that the facilitator is never permitted to impinge on the participants' process of forming their own judgements by steering the dialogue through uttering their own opinions. However, if the group members – through long schooling in Socratic Dialogue – are in a position to act in accordance with the rules, the work of facilitation can be dispensed with and the facilitator can participate in the content dialogue. Heckmann himself reported on such a dialogue. Normally facilitators hold back on matters of content because most groups need facilitator help. Giving this help is demanding and prevents the simultaneous participation on the content level.

Gustav Heckmann devotes one whole chapter to the problem of steering the dialogue. He understands 'steering' as measures through which the facilitator guides the dialogue in fruitful directions or prevents it from running into sand. Through these measures the facilitator steers the route taken by the group in addressing the topic in hand. In this sense, every action of the facilitator that attempts to influence participants to give attention to a particular sub-question or point, to discuss or not discuss these, is steering. Measures of steering which the group cannot be aware of or cannot penetrate are rejected. Equally, it is not acceptable that the facilitator should prejudge the issue, thus preventing participants from independently discovering an insight. Positive steering is present when the group recognises the reasons given by the facilitator for the suggestions put forward and then makes its own decision. Jos Kessels has named phases when the group considers and decides about the further direction of the dialogue as the 'strategy dialogue'.

The tasks of the facilitator and also the work of the group can be fulfilled more easily when important elements of the discussion are recorded in writing and thus constantly in full view. The important elements include significant aspects of the example, central arguments, statements of consensus, questions that are still to be addressed. The written record will include everything that the facilitator, the group or an individual participant wishes to have recorded. The writing up can be done by either the facilitator or another member of the group or on a rota basis.

The various tasks here ascribed to facilitators and the measures at their disposal should foster in the group the gaining of deeper insights and convictions founded on reason. They should also assist the group in their work towards consensus about the original question or statement or parts of that question or statement. It follows that the central responsibility of the facilitator is to spare no effort in helping the group to reach consensus. Heckmann states that:

> It is natural not to be content with the stage reached in the dialogue as long as there remain differences about a particular question, or as long as all participants have not yet agreed a

given statement. In a Socratic Dialogue we want to get beyond mere subjective opinion. That is why we seek out what reasons we have for our statements and then establish whether these reasons are acknowledged as being sufficient by all participants. Central to Socratic Dialogue is the search for meaning beyond the purely subjective, to strive for valid inter-subjective statements, for truth, as we used to say without hesitation.

Socratic Dialogue and the theory of knowledge

It would be naïve to assume that in a Socratic Dialogue we could discover the absolute truth. Nelson was convinced that one could formulate philosophical truth in a scientific manner. Mathematics was his model. Heckmann's position was different:

> Whenever we reach consensus about a statement in a Socratic Dialogue it has a provisional character. For the moment there are no further doubts about the outcome of our effort. Yet a point of view not previously noted can come into our awareness and arouse new doubts. In such a case the proposition has to be tested anew. No statement that emerges can ever avoid the need for further revision. [...] In Socratic Dialogue we strive for the possible and the sought after consensus always has the character of the provisional.

The foundation for the philosophical insight that can be won through Socratic Dialogue is the experience of the individual participant. We could understand this insight in terms of subjective conviction or absence of any further doubts. The fact that all experience is incomplete and new experiences can lead to new insights causes Heckmann to assert that in a Socratic Dialogue so-called definitive answers and irrefutable results cannot be found. This applies to all areas of human thought and research. This understanding is shared – according to my experience – by all Socratic facilitators. Socratic Dialogue is not yet underpinned by an agreed theory of knowledge. However, attempts are currently in progress to lay such a foundation, and in the circle of those interested in Socratic Dialogue there is an ongoing discussion in which the following questions are being raised:

- What is still valid in Nelson's theory of truth?

- Does discourse theory offer a possible approach?

- Can constructivism contribute something here?

Despite the fact that these questions about the theory of knowledge underlying Socratic Dialogue remain open, the intention here has been to offer an outline definition of it, to throw light on the choice of topics, to specify the rights and responsibilities of participants. The Socratic Dialogue is not an unrealistic proposal, neither is it fiction, nostalgia, or utopia. It has for the last seventy years been philosophy in practice, which year after year has been experienced by a growing number of people in different places.

Meta-dialogue

The above outline of contemporary Socratic Dialogue practice would be incomplete without reference to the meta-dialogue. This dialogue form was developed in the 1970s and is now a regular additional part of Socratic Dialogues. It is not part of the content dialogue in which the group works on a specific question or statement and is clearly separated from this. The agenda of the meta-dialogue is the behaviour of the group. Its purpose is to reduce any disturbances in the content dialogue. The needs and interests of the participants determine what is discussed. They could, for example, raise issues about the work in the group with which they were dissatisfied. This might refer to the conduct of individual participants or to that of the facilitator. It might also concern the ponderous, unproductive and confusing nature of the dialogue the reasons for which they have not yet identified. They ask themselves how such defects can be minimised and reflect whether possibly they have not kept to the Socratic rules. In addition, the group may express pleasure about a really successful dialogue and it can then clarify why the dialogue was so successful.

The sole purpose of the meta-dialogue is to support the work in the content dialogue. This is achieved through making the dialogue more transparent and by agreeing what changes in the behaviour of the group could improve the content dialogue. The group can, in addition, decide on how to proceed in the content dialogue. One has to avoid the participants turning themselves into a self-awareness group and evoking expectations that their therapeutic needs could be met.

During the meta-dialogue the special position of the facilitator is suspended. Her or his behaviour is open to criticism on an equal footing with others in the group. Normally, a member of the group with experience of Socratic Dialogue chairs the meta-dialogue.

As a matter of regular practice, or when there is an evident need for it, the group engages in a meta-dialogue. In a residential programme of several days it is usual to timetable a meta-dialogue in the afternoon, following an intensive Socratic Dialogue during the morning. Should there be a strongly felt need for a meta-dialogue, which is preventing concentrated work of a philosophical or mathematical nature become apparent during the content dialogue, the Socratic Dialogue is interrupted until the stumbling block has been removed.

Four indispensable features of Socratic Dialogue
It is likely that over time a more complete theoretical foundation will emerge and probably a further development of Socratic practice will occur. Such developments would have to be validated in the light of four indispensable features, which would have to be present in order to describe the dialogue as genuinely Socratic in the Nelson-Heckmann tradition.

1. *Starting with the concrete and remaining in contact with concrete experience*: insight is gained only when in all phases of a Socratic Dialogue the link between any statement made and personal experience is explicit. This means that a Socratic Dialogue is a process that concerns the whole person.

2. *Full understanding between participants*: this involves much more than verbal agreement. Everyone has to be clear about the meaning of what has just been said by testing it against her or his own concrete experience. The limitations of individual personal experience which stand in the way of full understanding should be called into consciousness and thereby transcended.

3. *Adherence to a subsidiary question until it is answered*: in order to achieve this the group is required to bring great commitment to their work and to gain self-confidence in the power of reason. This means, on the one hand, not giving up when the work is difficult, but on the other, to be calm enough to accept, for a time, a different course in the dialogue in order then to return to the subsidiary question.

4. *Striving for consensus*: this requires an honest examination of the thoughts of others and being honest in one's own statements. When such honesty and openness towards one's own

and other participants' feelings and thinking are present, then the striving for consensus will emerge, not necessarily the consensus itself.

The firm establishment of these four indispensable features of Socratic Dialogue tells us much about the tasks and behaviour of those who participate in such dialogues. The most important point in all this is the autonomy in thinking: only those who engage in the process of knowing in their own mind gain philosophical insights. External influences should do no more than stimulate independent thinking.

PART II
Experience in schools

4

THE CHALLENGE OF SOCRATIC DIALOGUE IN EDUCATION

Tamsyn Imison

This chapter describes the contribution of dialogue, including Socratic Dialogue, in the internal development of Tamsyn Imison's school, a large and successful comprehensive secondary school in inner London. She relates her experiences of introducing Socratic Dialogue to students in her school. The dialogues were facilitated by Rene Saran, who reports on them in chapters 7 and 8. Imison shows the significance Socratic Dialogue can have for the development of ethical awareness and competence among staff and students in a school.

Schools as learning communities

I was headteacher of a large successful comprehensive school in inner London from 1984 to 2000. We became a community of all students, teachers, support staff, governors, parents and community, who believed in, talked together about, and worked towards creating exciting learning environments where everyone would be both challenged and supported to continuously improve on their previous best. In other words, a true comprehensive school/community learning centre. Gadamer's perception (Hans-Georg Godamer, *Truth and Method*, 1998) of the importance of dialogues in bringing in new and improved understandings is more likely to be reflected when conversations about practice and learning are the norm, and there is much team teaching and sharing of practice. This became a non-elitist model of successful practice and openly challenged the 'refined' selective and specialist systems that are encouraged by the present government. It fits with the views of John Rawls' *Theory of Justice* (1971) and his views on equality of opportunity. Our credo became 'Learning Together Achieving Together' and this meant that we emphasised that everyone was expected to be a learner. We were wholly overt about the learning process and there was a good deal of talk about learning between teachers.

I became aware of the development and importance of having a strong learning focus in the mid 1990s when I was studying for a Masters in Education with the Open University. In my own learning explorations I noticed many other colleagues on similar journeys. Our conversations often led to pedagogical and system changes that improved learning for some students. But this was still a piecemeal approach that did not really tackle whole teams and certainly could not be said to have developed a learning community. There were also important excluded groups – those with young children, the carers and the financially constrained as well as the growing group of support staff whose contributions had yet to be fully realised or maximised.

In 1997/8 we established an in-house Masters programme with the Institute of Education, University of London for fifteen colleagues. This core group upped the quality of 'talk' and reflection about learning between teachers, as well as between teachers and students. Our credo, 'Learning Together, Achieving Together', became a reality and was known and understood by everyone. We used the valuable process of Investors in People to ensure we truly supported the professional learning of all staff and gained Investors status for the first time in 1998.

I was extremely fortunate in my first chair of governors, Dr Rene Saran, who brought me into the Society for the Furtherance of the Critical Philosophy. Founded in Germany by the Kantian philosopher, Leonard Nelson, this society aims to promote critical philosophy through the linked activities of education and scholarship. It is committed to engage a significant number in rigorous searching for the truth and in ethical issues based upon practical everyday problems using Socratic Dialogue and shared published research.

Our school council was trained in using Socratic Dialogues to discuss ethical issues of concern to them. All who participated expressed the view, in their evaluations, that it was a significant learning and enlightening experience. Students at Hampstead are actively engaged in formulating and reviewing whole school policy including the behaviour policy. No member of staff is appointed unless they have been seen in action by and approved by students in the school. All students are treated as rational adults.

Staff learning has been greatest when working together on challenging practice and researching into better ways of working. One of my personal best weekends of dialogue was an exploration of prime numbers with some of my maths staff, a tutor from the University of North London and a German professor of mathematics. There is a culture in the school of colleagues enjoying many social and active recreational experiences together and often also with students, as on the music and art expeditions as far afield as New York, Florence, Strasbourg and Barcelona. All teams, including the senior team, have had regular residential strategy weekends that have significantly improved learning and practice. This active engagement of students, staff, governors and others, including our important partners in higher education, significantly affected our ways of working within the school. I believe, from my own experience and from observing others engaged in learning, that learners often learn best collectively. This is a co-constructivist view and approach to learning (Heather Kanuka, *Philosophical Orientations in Instructional Technology*, 1999) where knowledge is negotiated through group conversations and dialogues. Knowledge and meaning as well as skills are shared and that then turns it into a changed external reality.

We renamed homework as independent learning and our library was upgraded into an independent learning centre. This has given far more open access for parents and the community. We all learnt and used technology to assist us with our own learning, to support higher-order thinking skills and as a means to open in-depth explorations into all areas of knowledge and skills. In order to finance the required new technologies we made two successful bids to develop the school as a specialist technology school, which did not distort the curriculum but used the technologies to deliver the whole curriculum. Knowledge and skills in using technologies were in turn delivered through all areas of the curriculum. We profoundly believe that young people need a broad and balanced curriculum until they are at least sixteen so they are given access to the same course of study for all, as set out in Mortimer J. Adler's *The Paideia Proposal*, 1982. This states that 'Schooling should open the doors to the world of learning and provide guidelines for exploring it'. It maintains that 'There are no unteachable children. There are only schools, teachers and parents who fail to teach them'. We have tried to ensure a balance between the three ways of supporting students' learning by reducing the number of didactic instructional lectures and responses and increasing use of coaching and exercises. We have supported independent learning as one might see in any group actively involved with new technologies, and used group seminars as well as dialogues with Socratic questioning and active participation.

We had what I call a 'DIM' goal – Demanding, Imaginative and Moveable – that no student would be turned off learning at the age of sixteen and everyone would want to go on to become a lifelong learner. By the early 1990s we had virtually achieved this. It was realised by everyone feeling valued and special while also being challenged to continuously improve on their personal best by regular discussions on strategies for improving learning and overcoming setbacks.

Our methodology has aimed to emulate Jerome Bruner's view (*The Culture of Education*, 1996) that 'we become ourselves through others'. Bruner says that 'the problem is not with competence but with performance. It is not that the child does not have the capacity to take another's perspective, but rather that he cannot do so without understanding the situation in which he is operating.' We can only understand if we converse and share to develop such understandings. In the words of Paulo Freire (*Pedagogy of the Oppressed*, 1993): 'To be an act of knowing, learning demands among teachers and students a relationship of authentic dialogue.'

5

SOCRATIC DIALOGUE IN TEACHING ETHICS AND PHILOSOPHY: ORGANISATIONAL ISSUES

Rene Saran and Barbara Neisser

This chapter presents an overview of the organisational and practical conditions needed for the successful introduction of Socratic Dialogue in ethics lessons in schools. The different stages of the dialogue, the meta-dialogue and the changed role of the teacher are outlined.

Teachers and successful Socratic facilitation
Many teachers in the twenty-first century have to teach new curriculum topics, such as personal, social and moral education, citizenship and ethics. These newer curriculum areas are often taught as an alternative to religious education. But the question arises as to how teachers can cope, given the different and often inadequate training provision, and the frequently changing legal requirements in some countries. We suggest here that the Socratic Method could help teachers who have to teach courses for students who are withdrawn from religious education lessons in order to attend alternatives such as social and moral education.

So what are the difficulties in school for which teachers acting as Socratic facilitators – or who integrate elements of the Socratic approach into their practice – need to be prepared? If the introduction of Socratic Dialogue in their school is to be successful, certain things are important.

In countries like the Netherlands, Britain and Germany it is evident that conditions are often favourable to the introduction of Socratic Dialogue. Relationships between students and staff are sufficiently relaxed and open for students and teachers to cope well with the challenge of participating in such a dialogue. In countries where hierarchy in schools is still entrenched, however, the situation is likely to be much more difficult. No one teacher can achieve the introduction of Socratic Dialogue alone. There must be a supportive environment within the school.

Certainly regard has to be paid to the wider environment: the stage the school is at; how much support there is (or could be developed) for trying Socratic Dialogue with some groups of children; the multicultural nature of the school; the expectations and attitudes among parents and the local community; the trust among students and staff to ensure confidentiality is respected when, for example, a student openly shares a delicate situation with a group.

Children and students need to develop social skills, but the creation of opportunities for this should be part of a school's task anyway. Listening skills, tolerant attitudes and the ability to be articulate are all necessary for the success of a Socratic Dialogue, but they are also valuable life skills. Schools and teachers can support children in developing these. Especially when working with younger children, it is important that the position of the teacher is not undermined. The teacher has the knowledge and is an authority. Introducing Socratic Dialogue might even be harmful in challenging teacher authority, making it difficult for the teacher to cope in the classroom and to maintain discipline.

As equality of all participants in a Socratic Dialogue is essential, this clearly challenges the entrenched hierarchy that has existed in many schools for 50 years or more – and still exists. As facilitator, the teacher is still an authority – insisting on discipline and tolerance in the group. There is a difference between conducting a Socratic Dialogue with an adult group and with one in a school. A schoolteacher has to manage the social behaviour of group members and ensure that conflicts between children are resolved in a tolerant manner, that is, that acceptance of differing viewpoints prevails. What the teacher would not do in a Socratic Dialogue is to give information or deliver a package of knowledge.

In Socratic Dialogue, the children have to be guided by the teacher in their journey of independent self-discovery, and towards understanding. This is an unusual role within school, as teachers are so often associated with conveying or teaching knowledge. A Socratic Dialogue might make students examine their basic beliefs and they might find this threatening. On the other hand students could experience a deepening of their knowledge about ethics and understand better how to deal with practical problems and questions. An important consideration is whether the questions for a Socratic Dialogue need to be screened, thus effectively limiting topics. The best approach is probably for children to formulate their questions together with their teacher.

Four phases in conducting a Socratic Dialogue
For work in schools the structure of the dialogue is here presented in a simplified form. We briefly describe four phases of a Socratic Dialogue and indicate what can be achieved in each phase. Such a division into phases is put forward as a guiding framework, from the perspective first and foremost of the facilitator.

The structure of a Socratic Dialogue is mainly determined by work with a concrete example. Ethical questions and problems are investigated by using a concrete example, drawn from the participants' experience. The example is not merely portrayed but is central to the way the whole discussion evolves. On the one hand analysis of the example throws up ethical questions and problems; on the other its everyday relevance and practical consequences are revealed.

Thus one avoids a situation where the discussion loses itself in general speculation and solutions to ethical conflicts are sought and found only at an abstract level. Furthermore, learners gain constant insights into the link between general ethical questions and their everyday experience and are able to use their philosophical reflection to guide individual action. Even at the stage when participants seek general insights and norms, the example remains central to testing the validity of general ethical statements and demonstrating their practical significance.

Phase 1
- Announcement of the Socratic Dialogue and choice of topic
- Fixing external conditions like time and rules
- Arrangements for report-writing
- Explanation of the meta-dialogue – when, how frequent, how long and under whose chairmanship
- Search for suitable examples as first step of the substantial / content discussion

Phase 2
- Choice of example by group or by facilitator
- Precise description of the example by the example-giver
- Questions by other participants, clarification of unclear elements, possibly also of relationship to topic
- Writing up of example

Phase 3
- Analysis of example: participants put questions to example-giver, make statements about actions and people in the example, express judgements about actions and raise problems about the example from their perspective
- Participants seek reasons for the actions and attitudes of people in the example – they ask the example-giver for reasons and agree with the discovered reasons or formulate alternative reasons
- Participants ask questions and investigate the norms and values that underpinned the actions of people in the example
- Participants identify points in the analysis of the example on which they agree
- The facilitator records the group's consensus

Phase 4
- Regressive abstraction: abstraction from the concrete example, investigation of general questions and problems which appear in the example

- Investigation of values and norms which determine the behaviour of people in the example; testing the extent to which these values and norms are ethically valid on the basis of reasons given

- Participants identify which abstractions gained from the example they can agree with

- Participants clear up points of conflict

- Participants formulate the shared insights they have reached

The meta-dialogue

Although Socratic Dialogue is a structured method, in reality it is not always easy to practise it. Making a protocol (a written report) can assist the group to establish a common starting point for the next session. Much patience, empathy and discipline in the dialogue are essential within the group. Group dynamic tensions may disturb the work and lead to conflicts.

In order to free the substantial or content dialogue from such disturbances and conflicts, these should be dealt with in a separate meta-dialogue. Normally each Socratic Dialogue will be accompanied by a meta-dialogue. However, at school one can also use the meta-dialogue as a starting point for a lesson, as it affords an opportunity to clear up questions on organisation and problems of understanding. Should there be disciplinary problems or difficult group dynamic tensions during the lesson, one can immediately interrupt the main dialogue to clear up these difficulties in a meta-dialogue.

Both participants and facilitator can ask for a meta-dialogue. This enables students once more to reflect at a different level on their own behaviour, on the arguments that have been used and the results that have been achieved. During this process the learners often address the issue of emotions, individual difficulties in understanding or questions of group dynamics. The assurance that there is this institutionalised opportunity to air these problems results, according to our experience, in willingness of participants – during the main dialogue – to concentrate and argue out the topic in a disciplined way.

Essential conditions for success

A Socratic Dialogue presupposes that certain organisational arrangements are in place. This is not always the case in school. Such arrangements may materially influence the success or otherwise of a Socratic Dialogue. The group needs several lessons per week to work on an ethical problem or a philosophical question. A double lesson is even better for one of the Socratic phases. Theme and project weeks are most suitable for longer Socratic phases.

The normal school timetable decrees short lessons. For Socratic Dialogue longer periods are needed, as for example, for group project work which is already a familiar practice in many secondary schools. Blocks of time over five to six weeks have proved valuable. Rene Saran's experience with secondary students is that half a school day (say a four-hour morning with a half hour break) was as much as the students could manage on one day, because the concentration required to listen and participate exhausted them. It also works well to have shorter periods (for example, a double lesson) twice a week. Group members could be expected to keep a Socratic diary for homework, the next lesson commencing with reading aloud one of the diaries or reports, thus achieving continuity in the group's work.

If possible the number of students should not exceed fifteen. Socratic Dialogues which take more than four weeks are difficult to integrate into the planning of lessons, which require a variety of methods to be used.

Ideally, every Socratic lesson should result in the writing of a report either by one student alone or by each student individually. The facilitator should also write a report. The writing of reports or the keeping of Socratic discussion diaries can be a meaningful homework exercise. Individual insights and central arguments can be recorded, as well as individual questions and comments on the dialogue topic. It is important to present these at the beginning of each new session, so that facilitator and learners together find a common starting point for continuing their topic.

The role of teachers in a Socratic Dialogue

Facilitators do not intervene in the substance of arguments but instead guide discussion. Normally facilitators prepare themselves intensively for Socratic Dialogue. They read around and reflect upon central aspects of the topic. In this way they construct for themselves an intellectual map of the various dimensions of the topic. Sometimes they reflect on examples drawn from their own everyday experience, or they prepare by engaging in a dialogue with another person with whom they can explore the various facets of the topic.

The aim of such preparation is to feel at home with the chosen topic. But facilitators should not give preference to any one aspect of the topic or impose preconceptions or presuppositions on the students in any way. Nor should facilitators be entrenched in particular philosophical theories or schools but should draw on these only for their own information. What counts during the preparation for and the leading of the dialogue are the basic principles: begin with actual experience; be open to the dialogue on the topic; let the group of learners decide which aspects of the topic are taken up and worked on.

During the process of choosing an example, facilitators can recognise, in light of their preparation, whether a given example is suited for a particular aspect of the topic. They are able to assess the complexities of the example and anticipate what generalised insights may be extracted from working with it.

During the analysis of the example and the process of abstraction that follows, it is the task of facilitators to be watchful that the group keeps to the question being investigated. They must lead the group to ensure that mutual understanding develops. A group can easily become confused if different aspects of the example are explored simultaneously or if students formulate unclear statements. Facilitators constantly need to foster clarity by ensuring that contributions are understood and perhaps by reminding the group of what has already been said.

Facilitators have several instruments at their disposal to steer the discussion. They can pose pointed questions and ask for contributions to the dialogue to be repeated. They can encourage group members to reformulate contributions already made by others. And they can summarise what has so far been achieved in the dialogue or briefly sketch the formal development of arguments and point to alternative paths open to the group.

During all phases of the discussion facilitators will seek to ensure that participants give their own judgements about the example. They will frequently request participants to check whether they agree with judgements made by others. Making judgements and validating them in terms of underpinning reasons are central to Socratic Dialogue. Essentially the dialogue involves a process of clarification and self-enlightenment about which reasons underpin our own judgements and whether these reasons are ethically valid and generalisable.

At school and during lessons teachers are normally experts in their subject and have authority on questions of content. Initially, when a teacher exercises restraint as a facilitator during the Socratic Dialogue, this is a new experience for students. However, students can be appropriately prepared and through independent learning in groups they can appreciate the changed role of the teacher. Nevertheless, it makes sense for the teacher to make more explicit the various positions taken up by students or to clarify them appropriately.

In a school setting, it should normally be the teacher who presides over the meta-dialogue, and who has the opportunity to practise the normal teaching role whenever this is helpful for the further development of the dialogue.

Practice in England, Wales and Germany

The structures of school systems are complex and are not described here. There is no requirement to teach ethics as such in English or Welsh schools. Nevertheless, ethical topics are likely to be developed in some or all of the following, which are required by law:

- A daily act of collective worship
- Personal, social, moral and cultural education
- Citizenship (part of the national curriculum in secondary schools)
- Religious education (for which arrangements are determined locally)
- School policies

Schools which know about the Socratic Method have considerable freedom to use it as one way to raise awareness of ethical issues, thus contributing to the students' personal, moral, social and cultural education, and to the other aspects of school life.

Daily act of worship (school assembly)
Since the 1988 Education Reform Act, now incorporated in the 1996 Education Act, schools must provide daily collective worship for all registered pupils up to age eighteen (unless withdrawn by their parents). The daily act of worship must be wholly or mainly of a broadly Christian character. Where the headteacher and governing body of a school consider such an act of worship unsuitable, the head may apply to the local Standing Advisory Council for Religious Education to have the Christian content requirement lifted. The Department for Education and Skills then needs to endorse alternative provision.

Personal, social, moral and cultural education
All schools must provide such education. Most schools do so through lessons in personal and social education, or in personal, health and social education. But schools have discretion over the means of delivery of this requirement. Provision is likely to be informal as well as formal.

Citizenship
In 2002, an Act of Parliament made it compulsory for all secondary schools to teach citizenship but it is optional for primary schools. The syllabus is expected to cover topics such as government, parliament, citizen rights, and skills for active citizenship.

Religious education
It is a national requirement under law that the subject religious education is offered. However, parents may withdraw their children. For Local Education Authority schools, a local standing advisory council for religious education determines the syllabus. Most advisory council outlines for religious education involve the study of world religions. In many areas humanist groups are represented on the local advisory council alongside religious interests. Thus religious education lessons usually deal with different belief systems and customs rather than asserting what should be believed. In denominational schools the deciding body is the local diocesan authority, or appropriate religious body.

School policies
Schools have considerable autonomy to develop their own policies. Nevertheless, they are required by law (School Standards

and Framework Act 1998) to secure good behaviour in line with general principles drawn up by the school's governing body. Headteachers have a legal obligation to implement measures to prevent all forms of bullying and all discrimination on grounds of gender, race and religion. Schools have to have and to implement an equal opportunities policy and the Race Relations (Amendment) Act 2000 has placed a statutory obligation on them to prevent and address racism. Sex education must be provided in secondary schools, but in primary schools it is optional.

These various requirements, all of which raise ethical issues, are often supplemented by school and classroom codes of conduct, and can provide opportunities for topics for Socratic Dialogue.

In Germany, children over fourteen years old may decide for themselves whether or not they want to take part in religious education or participate instead in ethics or in practical philosophy. In several of the federal states (*Bundesländer*) the law specifies various detailed requirements not described here. Ethical issues and problems are likely to be dealt with in German schools in some or all of the following subjects:

- Religious education
- Ethics, values and norms or practical philosophy for younger age groups
- Philosophy for older students
- Subjects such as social science, science of education, history

Ethics and religious education
Ethical issues are part of religious education in all years. The two important aspects are the specific content of Christian ethics including the differences between the Protestant and Roman Catholic churches, and actual ethical problems and personal moral views.

Ethics, values and norms or practical philosophy
The central topics of the alternative forms of moral and ethical education, in common with religious education, are questions concerning values and general principles of behaviour. Young people learn to understand and accept the pluralism of religion and cultures and of different views of the world. They also learn to

base their ethical views on rational arguments and to become sensitive to social and ethical questions. Attention is given to moral orientation, personal responsibility, and the ability to reflect on moral problems and judgements. Ethics is given a mainly practical meaning. The lessons aim to foster individual moral behaviour and to secure personal behaviour in line with the general principles of the democratic constitution.

Ethics as part of philosophy
For older students, ethics is included with philosophy and is more developed. In addition to personal development, moral judgement and social education, philosophy also involves learning about different cultural and philosophical positions and finding reasons for moral principles, ethical norms and values. The law requires that teaching not be biased in any way towards particular denominations or world views. Teachers are required to respect human values, altruistic behaviour and ethical universalism. Humanism and ethical universalism in Europe mean all people are equal under the law as regards race, gender, religion and social origin.

Ethics as part of social science
In the range of social science subjects, ethics is incorporated in particular topics. It is a requirement that the ethical competence of students is furthered and developed across all subjects. The general regulations for the sixth form oblige students to deal with 'values, systems of values and ethical principles of behaviour', in order 'to find reliable answers to the meaning of life'. Students are expected to engage in activities of a social character, and are to be assisted with participation as citizens in a democratic society.

6

EXPERIENCES WITH SOCRATIC DIALOGUE IN PRIMARY SCHOOLS

Ingrid Delgehausen

> Ingrid Delgehausen's experiences in conducting Socratic Dialogues in a German primary school with children aged seven and older demonstrates that Socratic Dialogue can be used to encourage children to philosophise. The children become more self-confident and aware of ethical problems in their relationships with others.

For many years I have been a teacher at a primary school in Lower Saxony, catering for children between six and about ten. The experiment of facilitating Socratic Dialogues began during religious education with children aged seven upwards. I allowed aspects of that form of dialogue to become part of class conversation. I was astonished to find that even large groups (up to 22 children) were more easily and better prepared for communicating with each other than when I taught them by means of question and answer.

As a result of practical experience in facilitating Socratic Dialogues with juveniles and adults elsewhere, I felt encouraged to conduct that kind of conversation with children in my school. After the first few sessions my reservations about group size, discipline and the ability of children to be both articulate and able to engage in abstract thinking, were overcome. I conducted Socratic

Dialogues in four different groups and under different conditions. The results varied, but all of them were positive.

I offered the first dialogue to children aged seven as a voluntary additional group activity. The school authorities approved their being held in school. The pupils showed interest and brought written agreement from their parents, permitting them to participate in Socratic Dialogue for an hour after their regular lessons. I had mentioned in advance that I preferred groups of ten. As out of 25 children eighteen declared interest, we had no choice but to draw lots in order to keep the number down to ten participants. The ratio between boys and girls corresponded to that in their class. Thus, following the drawing of lots, three girls and seven boys took part. The advantage we enjoyed with this group was that we only met when all the children were actually able to attend. If a child fell ill, a chain of telephone calls was set in motion the evening before or on the morning of the designated day, notifying parents that school for their children would end at the usual time. In the course of a school year we had thirteen sessions of 45 minutes each.

I had previously proposed to the children the subject 'What is friendship?' At the first session I explained, in appropriate language, the six measures or rules of Socratic Dialogue described in his book by Gustav Heckmann. I wrote them on the blackboard in short slogans. I gave a copy of any notes written on the blackboard, as well as a brief report, to each child at the beginning of the next lesson. I did not demand any writing by the children, since at that age most of them still had considerable difficulty with spelling when copying, as well as with writing quickly.

At the beginning of each lesson the report of the previous session was read out in turn by the children, to refresh their memory and facilitate entry into the next dialogue.

In the second session, each child gave at least one example to illustrate the subject. Each described a brief situation in which he or she had experienced friendship. To my astonishment these young children were often much better than adults at identifying the main point in their example.

They produced brief and concise accounts, giving flashes of insight into their experiences in a way I had never experienced with older participants. Friends to whom I later related this phenomenon (which was repeated in other groups) thought that this was because children did not yet have the wealth of experience of older people. I do not believe that. My impression was that they were emotionally less burdened. It was much easier for them to accept the rules and observe them than it is for adults. They had no need to project themselves during the dialogues. They were 'more equal' among themselves than is the case with adults.

The choice of the example was quick and straightforward, so that in subsequent sessions good work in the matter of content progressed without delay. After a few weeks of work the children's statements were also tested against other examples and, in fact, early steps were taken in abstraction. It was clear to the children that their reasoned views needed to stand up also in other situations. Initially we always wrote 'All' instead of using the concept 'consensus'. After some time, I introduced this notion, and the children discovered many criteria for the understanding of the concept 'friendship'. They tested differentiated statements, examined them, rejected or approved them, but were always openminded. On the final day they reached their last consensus: 'Although we don't yet know precisely what friendship is, we have discovered many 'things' that most definitely belong to friendship.'

Most of the time every child tried hard to observe the rules of the dialogue, to move the topic forward, to stand up for his or her own opinion. Once, when writing a statement down on the blackboard, I made a slight mistake; one of the boys immediately corrected me: 'Frau Delgehausen, you said one should never say 'yes' if one thinks differently from the others. So I have to tell you that you have written down a wrong word and not my sentence.' Often they also tried to repeat the statements of their classmates in words of their own without my having to ask them to do so. Thus their sentences often began with: 'If I understood Tina correctly, she meant ...', or 'I think Anika is trying to say that ...', or 'Did I correctly understand you to say ...?'. Before reflecting on what their comment would be, they first tried to understand precisely what the other person had tried to say. We adults often have so many compartmentalised categories in our heads that we have already assigned and criticised a statement before we have fully understood it. The children were far less biased and handled this much more easily, for they had fewer inhibitions in expressing themselves.

In one of the first sessions a boy started crying. The others were so engrossed in the conversation that they had not yet noticed it. I asked him the reason for his tears. He replied that he was so sad because he had no new ideas and his name was not yet on the blackboard. Until then I had always taken care, if at all possible, to have all children's names and their statements on the blackboard. I now explained to them that Socratic Dialogue is a communal effort and that the names were not there to denote praise but merely to remind us who had said what. We then spoke about the concept of consensus and that we – the group – were always only as far along as every one of us was at that point.

A few words are needed about the meta-dialogue in the first group. Initially I wondered whether to conduct any meta-dialogue at all. The children were obviously feeling happy and were truly working splendidly with one another. Any real problem, like the boy who felt left out on the board, we dealt with on the spot. Nevertheless, I decided to have a brief meta-dialogue at the end of each lesson. Certain observations I found very amusing:

Sebastian: I think it stupid that the time is always over so quickly

Alexander: The time goes as quickly as when I ride in the Ferrari from Lohnde to Seelze (about 1.5 km)

Tina: It all comes straight from the heart and not only from the head

Annika: It's great that I don't have to be afraid of saying something wrong and then get a poor grade

Frédéric: One doesn't always have to agree, but one should try to

There were certainly no quarrels and no references to insults such as sometimes occur in meta-dialogues between adults. Everyone told me how s/he had felt. For some of the children in this group the Socratic Dialogue had been, along with their sports lessons, the 'coolest' thing in school.

As I found my first experience of Socratic Dialogue with children to have been so positive I ventured further. For some years, I have offered Socratic Dialogue to nine-year-olds, within the framework of an activity session. Our school offers a variety of options (workshops) for that age group, such as knitting, making window pictures, music, flute playing, table tennis, drawing and painting. The children can choose between the different options. If groups are too big we split them to ensure that no more than ten children are being taught together. One drawback of the Socratic option was that from time to time a child was sick and therefore absent. However, as children were not absent too often, we were able to bring the child up to date with the missed dialogue by repeating the previous dialogue in the next lesson. A further difficulty was that, as a result of splitting the group up, I had the same children only once a fortnight. This meant a long gap between dialogue sessions and some pupils sometimes had difficulty in remembering it all. So I wrote the sentences on the blackboard again and photocopied them – which gave them much pleasure. No group, up to then, had any great wish themselves to copy what was written on the blackboard.

In both groups I again proposed the topic 'What is friendship?' The initial sessions took much the same course as with the first group. Later sessions revealed minor differences in attitude and results. One group consisted of girls only, another was mixed, but with more boys than girls. The girls' group sometimes had difficulties concentrating, listening to one another, and jointly seeking formulations. After a few sessions they noticed that they had reached consensus on fewer occasions than the other group. This disappointed them. Only after a meta-dialogue, when I had explained to them that I had felt unhappy at their interrupting each other, holding conversations on the side, showing lack of concentration, and told them that the number of instances of reaching consensus did not matter, did their attitude to the work change. Unfortunately, I had no concluding dialogues in either of the groups as the two periods were dropped for timetable reasons. Consequently these dialogues did not end as 'rounded off', as the first had done.

In the next year, Socratic Dialogues were again offered as an option for nine-year-olds. As this group included children from my previous class, with whom I had already conducted Socratic Dialogues, I did not propose a topic on this occasion. I explained to the pupils what kind of questions we could discuss in a Socratic Dialogue and gave them two suggestions:

- Are rules at school sensible?
- Order is half one's life

Then I asked them to think of questions themselves that interested them. The following questions were added:

- Should one never lie?
- Why should one protect the environment?
- Why does one sometimes have to ask questions?
- What does Jesus mean by 'love your neighbour like yourself'?

The pupils decided on the question: 'Why should one protect the environment?' Each child had two votes, and this question received a vote from every child, whereas the second vote was spread among several questions.

I always proceeded like this in the choice of the example. Unlike with adults there was never a problem with deciding on which of the examples to pursue.

I am very glad I dared to conduct the experiment of Socratic Dialogues with primary schoolchildren. My expectations were greatly exceeded. Both the children and myself had much fun and pleasure out of it. And I had the impression that all the children had gained something quite special, even though in the search for truth they advanced only by a few small steps and the insights they gained were limited. They experienced a different way of treating each other; the different atmosphere during the sessions; they gained practice in formulating statements, as well as enhanced self-assurance and self-determination – all these are positive results of our work.

7

SOCRATIC DIALOGUE – MY FIRST EXPERIENCE

Rene Saran

In her chapter, Tamsyn Imison referred to Rene Saran's work with students at Hampstead Comprehensive School. The aim was to enhance the thinking skills of students who had been elected to represent their classmates on the school council. This chapter has appeared previously as an article both in Britain and in Germany (for details *see* appendix 4).

Introduction

I have been a long-standing governor of Hampstead Comprehensive School in north west London. Another thread in my life is experience of the Socratic Method in both Germany and Britain. Some years ago, I talked to secondary headteachers in Camden, a borough in London, about the value this method might offer to secondary school students. The first Socratic Dialogue I facilitated in a school was at Hampstead School with ten girls and boys aged thirteen to sixteen. All were elected members of the school council, which from time to time reviews the school's rules and classroom code. I therefore suggested the topic 'Are rules necessary?' Most of this text is a report on the students' dialogue.

What Socratic Dialogue can offer

Students experience an opportunity to improve their critical thinking and reasoning skills by philosophising cooperatively in a group, aiming to arrive at agreement on a challenging question. The question is at the centre of the dialogue and is explored through systematic reflection about a concrete experience of one or more of the participants, with which all in the group can identify. Everyone in the group (in this case including the headteacher) has an equal right to be heard. The discussion moves slowly and systematically, so that all participants gain insight into the substance of the dialogue. The process of learning to philosophise moves from the concrete, particular experience to seeking general propositions, judgements or answers, validated by reasons which all in the group find convincing.

The Hampstead dialogue
It quickly became apparent that everyone in the group agreed that rules are indeed necessary, so a simple 'yes' answer could have concluded our activity. It did not take long to turn the question into a more challenging one, and the students made various suggestions:

- Are all rules necessary?
- When are rules necessary?
- In what circumstances are rules necessary?
- Why are rules necessary? The majority settled for this question

Finding an example
In the past I have worked with adult groups and I was immediately struck by the simple nature of the students' examples. Adults often have a way of making things more complicated. Every student briefly outlined an experience. Each example consisted of a discrete event. Most, but not all, related to school life. Two examples related to primary school, six to Hampstead School and three to experiences outside school:

1. At primary school we were not allowed fizzy drinks, but the teachers could have them

2. At junior school our uniform prescribed white ankle socks, otherwise we were sent home. It was ridiculous!

3. Even though it was cold in the classroom, I had to take off my jacket because of the classroom code

4. I was in physical education (PE). The teacher would not allow me to wear my hoops because of the PE code: no jewellery

5. We were late for the coach to go to off-site PE. But we were not allowed out of the year room until we had finished our lunch: no walking to the coach whilst eating

6. I asked a friend a relevant question during a maths lesson and was told to be quiet under the classroom code

7. We are not allowed to drink in the classroom. I was rushing to be on time for registration and could not finish my drink

8. On sports day our teacher required that equal numbers of girls and boys participate in each team. My team was unable to enter because we were short of girls

9. In a local meeting attended by potentially angry people, I felt the rules for the meeting ensured reasonable order

10. My age barred me from going on the bouncy castle at the fairground

11. Passes have to be shown on the bus. I am fifteen, but without my pass I had to pay the adult fare

Before deciding which example to choose for our dialogue, the group made two observations: firstly, that each example described a situation in which the person either questioned or confirmed a given rule; and secondly, that fairness in the application of rules appeared in many examples.

Thereafter, various examples were 'nominated', and reasons given for their choice. These included that certain rules about equality are of major importance and that some examples involved the interesting question of relationships between teachers and students. In the end two examples received an equal number of votes (numbers 1 and 8), so we chose 8 by tossing a coin! Next, we had to describe the example in more detail in order then to pursue the question: Why are rules necessary?

The selected example
At the recent Hampstead team sports day, boys (from the same class) outnumbered girls. For the tug-of-war the rule was that each team should have four boys and four girls. My class had only two girls and we were not allowed to borrow two additional girls

from another class. My team therefore entered four boys and two girls against another team of four boys and four girls. So we lost because we were disadvantaged. This was unfair because the rules were applied inflexibly.

Why are rules necessary?
The group returned to the main question and examined the rule concerning four boys and four girls per side by asking two relevant sub-questions:

- Why was the particular rule needed?
- Why was the rule applied so rigidly on sports day?

In answer to the first, participants agreed that an orderly competition requires rules. Further, that it is important to ensure equal sides, and that this equality could refer to boys/girls; athletes/non-athletes, and to balance between teams (which could be met, for example, by six boys and two girls per team).

Looking at the second question, the students found it puzzling that the four boys/four girls rule had been applied so inflexibly. They argued that in the application of rules all circumstances should be taken into account. In the example, this meant that note should have been taken of the fact that more boys than girls had turned up for sports day. The low turn out of girls may have resulted from stereotyping (for example, football is for boys not girls). Given the circumstances, rigid application of the rule meant pressure was put on the girls to participate in the event. This exhausted them and some of them almost literally hobbled into the headteacher's room, where the Socratic Dialogue took place.

Before the lunch break, then, our conclusion was that rules are needed for the orderly pursuit of team games, but that a more flexible application of the particular rule in our example would have been fairer and thus more acceptable.

New questions
After lunch it became clear that the morning's effort of listening and contributing to the dialogue had required great concentration. A certain weariness pervaded the room.

We therefore made a new start, using points that had arisen during the morning. Many of the original examples had referred to the classroom code, others to rules. It seemed almost as if the two terms were used interchangeably, and several students thought teachers applied the classroom code as if it were a set of rules. The question that aroused interest at this stage was: What is the difference between codes and rules? A subsidiary question was: Are codes more effective?

Several new thoughts were thrown into the arena. Maybe rules set out what one has to or must do. Such rules create barriers to permitted action. They spell out explicitly the dos and don'ts. Rules concerning safety in the science laboratories were cited. Maybe, then, by contrast, codes lay the basis for good behaviour, in the sense of providing guidance. Reference was made to the code of not wearing outdoor clothing in the classroom. One student had been told to take his jacket off on a very cold day, as if this were a rule to be rigidly applied.

By now, time was running out. One final question was repeated: Are codes or rules more effective? The group recognised that we had not made the distinction between codes and rules sufficiently clear, so we were unable to answer the question. But we did agree that both codes and rules are more effective if:

- those to whom they apply have been involved in making and amending them

and

- there is a good teacher/student relationship

Evaluation of the day by students

Students made the following points about their first experience of the Socratic Dialogue:

- It had heightened their listening skills

- It had increased their understanding of the teacher's situation

- It had focused and concentrated their thinking

- Participants had experienced different viewpoints on the same issue and the Socratic Dialogue had made them more considerate towards the viewpoints of others

- Systematic discussion of one topic is hard and requires great concentration

- The group had experienced mutual trust among all members
- They had enjoyed the work

To improve the activity for other groups of school students, two suggestions were put forward:

- The dialogue should be timetabled for the morning only
- Students should be involved in the choice of topic

The facilitator's reflections

The practice of the Socratic Dialogue has great potential for school students. Clearly it needs skilful facilitation – I know only too well that it is not easy to be a good facilitator. But the activity is very rewarding.

I would like to conclude with the comment that it was easy for the students aged thirteen to sixteen to move from the relatively simple concept of 'rule' to a much more complex one: 'flexibility of rule application'. This could be highly relevant to the question of teacher discretion in schools or, by analogy, to a judge's discretion in a court of law. The transition from the simple to the more complex concept came about because the students shared with the example-giver the feeling of unfairness. Ethical issues arose for them. In seeking to understand their shared feeling, the group thought that the rule about equal opportunity for boys and girls had been applied too inflexibly in the particular circumstances. The students discovered that inflexibility could lead to unfairness. They tried to address the issue of how to distinguish between rules that should be applied inflexibly and those where it might be valid, even desirable, to apply them flexibly.

They did not gain the insight that flexible application of rules might also lead to unfairness (for example, if differential sanctions were applied as between students for the same breach of a rule).

8
EXPERIENCES WITH SOCRATIC DIALOGUE IN SECONDARY SCHOOLS

Rene Saran

These previously unpublished accounts of several Socratic Dialogues facilitated by Rene Saran in comprehensive schools in two areas of London provide an overview of the examples with which the students worked, the questions they asked, and the questions which were investigated in greater depth. The outcomes achieved by students and their evaluation of participation in a Socratic Dialogue are discussed.

Introduction
Socratic Dialogues at London schools
The previous chapter provided a detailed account of a one-day Socratic Dialogue at Hampstead Comprehensive School. This chapter offers an overview of two further dialogues at Hampstead School organised by Tamsyn Imison, the then headteacher. Three more Socratic Dialogues were conducted in Greenwich, in south east London, as part of a cross-borough experiment. The co-ordinator for schools at borough level, Rasha Hammani, was responsible for the organisation of this pilot activity, which was intended to foster cross-borough cooperation between Greenwich secondary schools. Rasha Hammani was present at all three dialogues and acted as scribe for the facilitator.

The topics at Hampstead School were:

- Equal rights for girls and boys
- Is bullying a fact of life?

At the Greenwich schools one question was addressed by all groups, as the composition of the groups changed. This question was:

- How should a breach of school rules be dealt with?

Organisational arrangements

It proved beneficial to students to mix the group where possible, either by age or by school. Students enjoyed the stimulation and interest of working with young people from other classes or schools. Of the five dialogue groups reported on here, only one was made up of ten girls and boys aged twelve to thirteen years who were all from one class at one school. In this case some of the zest resulting from fruitful cross-fertilisation was conspicuously missing.

Another beneficial feature at the Hampstead School dialogues was that they were time-tabled for the morning only, following a recommendation made by students in the Socratic Dialogue covered in chapter 7. In Greenwich, the time-span embraced morning and part of the afternoon, with a lunch break. This was hard going for the students, as systematic discussion of a single topic requires great concentration. For the first hour, the students had worked with their own teachers, collecting examples, which were then presented to the whole group once the Socratic facilitator joined them.

Advance information had been distributed (although in a busy school this does not always reach the students who will attend!). Before beginning, the facilitator therefore had to check that everyone in the group understood the nature of the activity upon which they were about to embark.

Experience of these five Socratic Dialogues with school students confirmed that, in contrast to adults, young people very quickly present relevant examples for the dialogue. The early phase of presenting examples and choosing one or more to work with normally took no more than half an hour. In some cases common or contrasting features in the listed examples were identified, and the examples checked for suitability for the question to be answered. Sometimes the example was chosen by tossing a coin, as student preferences were divided – always providing, of course, that both possible examples were well suited to the group's work. Writing up the essential features of the chosen example on the flipchart was quickly accomplished. Not all groups chose only one example; in Greenwich the groups worked with more than one.

All five dialogues were structured in a roughly similar way, so they will be described in sequence under the following headings:

- Collecting and choosing examples
- Working with the chosen example(s) – asking subsidiary questions, making judgements, formulating reasons
- Reaching consensus
- Evaluation (for the Greenwich schools the points made during this phase are collected together at the end of the fifth dialogue report)

The first dialogue: equal rights for girls and boys
Collecting and choosing examples
In this half-day Socratic Dialogue each of the ten girls and boys aged thirteen to fifteen from the school council gave a quick example about school life. Most examples were about teachers treating girls differently from boys, but one concerned the way in which an all-boys class had treated a woman teacher differently from a male teacher – showing the woman less respect.

After brief reflection about all the examples given, the group chose one that was then written out more fully on the flipchart, as follows:

We were in a French lesson two years ago. Our teacher left the room for a brief period and the students started talking and walking round the classroom. One boy took a tape from the tape-player; a group of boys clustered around whilst the girls were watching and laughing. A window was opened and a boy threw the tape out. It so happened that a senior teacher was walking by. She was seen by some of the students – all the class quickly sat down. The girls sat nearest to the window.

The class teacher returned but did not realise what had happened. The senior teacher came up to the class and asked whether anyone knew who had thrown the tape out of the window. The students all put their heads down. The senior teacher then went all round and asked each student 'Was it you?' Nobody owned up although every student knew who had done it. The senior teacher then said the girls could leave. Some boys said to the senior teacher:

Why are the boys being kept in?

We, the boys, were not sitting by the window

Working with the chosen example
The student who gave the example was critical of the way the senior teacher had managed the situation. The facilitator encouraged her to express views about what had happened. She explained:

- I think the senior teacher should have kept the whole class back until the culprit was identified, even if she suspected someone among the boys
- I remember distinctly that the boys were very upset

Students resented the assumption made by the senior teacher that the culprit was a boy, before a proper investigation had been made. They saw this assumption as based on the view that boys misbehave more frequently than girls. This attitude had resulted in discrimination against the boys. The group then asked the following questions about the example:

1 *How* would I (we) have wanted the issue handled?

2 a) *Why* were the boys so upset?

  b) *Why* do we think that keeping the boys in the classroom was unfair?

At this point the facilitator probably drew attention to the fact that 'why?' questions (unlike 'how?' questions) lead to a process of reasoning, which is more likely to illuminate the issues at stake for the students. In any case, the group settled for question 2a.

The following answers and reasons were put forward by different students:

- The boys were upset because the chance of being blamed was increased and the chance of getting away with it was reduced

- The boys were segregated from the girls and judged before the evidence was available. They felt this was unjust

- The boys felt in their hearts that they were discriminated against because they were boys

- These boys were deprived of their right to be treated equally. They have been taught that discrimination on any grounds is wrong and now it was happening to them

- Usually gender discrimination is seen to be directed against females – but here the boys were experiencing discrimination because of being male. It often goes unnoticed when males are discriminated against

- Beyond the actual example, it was thought that stereotyping of boys and men is generally accepted. (The view was also expressed that questions of race have a much higher profile than those of gender.)

Reaching consensus

The students in this group agreed to summarise their learning as follows:

- Boys are just as much discriminated against as girls

- Much work still needs doing to achieve real equality between the sexes

- Girls are more aware of discrimination against themselves than boys are of discrimination against boys

- All of us should be more aware of what sexism actually is (we should be taught about it). This would reduce the number of incidents

- Boys are not willing to show when they are upset – they are afraid of being seen as weak

Evaluation
By the students
- The second half of the session was more interesting – once we started exploring the example

- The dialogue clarified our thinking about the issue
- Our participation in the dialogue will make us more active on the issue
- We experienced more focused thinking, deeper thinking
- We needed more time, once we had chosen our example
- In our course 'Self and Society' we could take back our experience
- The Socratic Dialogue could be applied to the topic of bullying (this topic was covered in the second dialogue, see the next report)

By the facilitator
The topic aroused much interest and the students were lively and articulate. Their headteacher sat among them as an equal participant. An atmosphere of excitement and discovery prevailed in the room and the students were keen that the Socratic Method be experienced by more students. In order to give everyone an equal chance to participate, groups should ideally be small (ten is a good number). The challenge remains to train more people to undertake this exciting work.

The second dialogue: is bullying a fact of life?
Collecting and choosing examples
On this occasion, the headteacher explained that the school wanted to offer the opportunity of participation in the dialogue to students in the younger age groups who still have plenty of time to put into practice what they learn during the Socratic activity. The school encouraged students to contribute actively to policy and good practice, and expected students to help each other and the staff to carry out the school's anti-bullying policy.

Again, this was a half-day Socratic Dialogue and nine of the ten girls and boys aged twelve to fourteen gave a personal example from school life of having been a victim of bullying. The examples covered issues such as name-calling, taking a friend away, degrading another person, physical hurt, threats and intimidation:

1. When I was seven, other kids on the estate where I lived called me racist names – they bullied me

2. People used to call me Demon when I was smaller (a play on the student's name). I did not like it. Were they bullying me?

3. In primary school I was called fat. This may be taken as an offence but I did not take it as such

4. Three friends in primary school – two had a special friendship and the third was jealous. She was nasty to me, bullied me

5. A boy at secondary school constantly commented on my appearance, made me feel really bad. He bullied me and others

6. A photo was taken of me, photocopied many times and displayed round school with nasty things written on it. Students were bullying me and I did not like it

7. At primary school the teacher was reading to us. A girl pulled my hair. She had called me names during break and took my friends away

8. Other students at secondary school said nasty things about our appearance and behaviour (referring to me and my friends). It stopped me going to certain parts of the school; I did not like it. Now I don't care. I am not nasty back

9. I had a row with another girl and thought it was finished. Next day she and a bigger group of boys and girls threatened me: 'We'll get you after school'. I was frightened for two weeks

On reviewing the above examples for their suitability for our further work unanimity was quickly reached. It was agreed to work with example 6. The girl whose photo had been displayed round the school agreed to be the example-giver. Her example was then fleshed out as follows:

Some students got hold of a photo of me. They photocopied it. They wrote nasty comments on some of the copies (slag, bitch). Some were stuck up in the corridor of the English block. A boy told me: 'These are being handed round school'. My sister and I threw a lot of them away. The action made me feel small, I had done nothing to the bullies. This time the bullying was the last straw and I had to tell the teachers again, this time saying something had to be done because I could not handle it anymore. Meanwhile I have learnt to cope, but I don't like the way the bullies get at my friends in order to get at me. The bullies are always in a group, which is threatening.

Working with the chosen example

Even before collecting the above examples, the facilitator had asked the group on this occasion to give a 'Yes' or 'No' answer to the question under discussion. It is one way to stimulate interest and to bring out a range of views at the very beginning of the dialogue. Some students gave provisional answers, and the views were summarised on the flipchart:

- Bullying is *not* a fact of life – people make it happen
- Bullying does not have to happen, but it does. It does not happen to everybody, nor is everyone a bully
- Everyone has a different experience of bullying
- Everyone gets teased sometime, but not everyone gets bullied (this raised the further question of what the difference is between teasing and bullying)
- There are two types of bullying: physical and verbal

Once the example was written up, the group suggested further questions and tried to answer the last one:

- Why did the bully (bullies) do it?
- Why is the bullying offensive?
- Is bullying mostly a group action?
- How can victims handle bullying (verbal abuse)?

The example-giver then explained to the group why she had been unable to cope with the photograph incident:

- She had already been bullied so often
- She was angry, which only intensified the situation because the bullies saw they were upsetting her and consequently they bullied her all the more
- The particular class she was in made her feel alone

The next step was to explore how the example-giver learnt to cope with the bullying situation. Again she gave a number of reasons:

- She now felt stronger and more confident
- Teachers now gave support, so she was no longer alone
- She was no longer angry, merely irritated

- She had moved to a new class and had new friends
- The bullied had changed their view of bullies – they had pity for them, which meant they no longer stooped to their level
- They knew a better life was possible

Reaching consensus

Having explored with the victim (the example-giver) the reasons why she had initially been unable to handle the bullying and had later learnt to cope with it, the group extended the discussion on a broader level, seeking to identify strategies for dealing with bullying. Students suggested that as they grew older, they and the bullies changed (the example-giver even added that the bullies are now her friends).

It helps to ignore the bullying, to be strong and appear to be strong, and to respond quickly, for example by showing anger. Enjoying oneself was also seen as a valuable strategy: if one has a lot of real friends with whom one could be sociable, laugh and talk, then one could laugh at how pathetic the bullies really are. 'Real friends', it was suggested, are people who stick by each other and will not be nasty to each other no matter what group settings they find themselves in.

By way of summary of the group's shared thoughts, a table of guidance was drawn up.

Guidance to Victims and Bullies

Victims	*Bullies*
1. Don't believe what the bully says you are	1. Learn how to grow up
2. Be aware of your own strengths (everyone has their own beauty)	2. Learn how to make real friends
3. Have or make real friends who: will back you up / with whom you can enjoy yourself / can tease each other, but not bully / we can trust / have a nice personality / are good people	3. Learn to laugh *with* not *at* people
4. Seek help (from teachers and other people whom we can trust)	4. Seek help on how not to bully

Evaluation
By the students
At the end, a quick gathering together of impressions of the Socratic Dialogue produced the following:

- We learnt about other people's experience
- It was good to hear other students' experience
- We see people in a different light, including bullies
- I found people agree with me – this builds confidence
- Participation in the SD has been a confidence builder
- I have been helped not to be scared any more and to help others
- We saw that bullies want something we have (eg real friends) – it is not just about superficial things like clothes
- We have learnt that we should not leave the situation for ages before tackling it
- We learnt how people cope with bullying
- We learnt that enjoyment and having real friends helps
- We have gone into the topic in greater depth, the time has gone quickly, we recognise that we need time to think and reflect

By the facilitator
It was striking and impressive that the students, entirely on their own, wanted to offer guidance not only to victims but also to bullies. This group displayed much imagination, understanding and willingness to help each other through difficult situations.

The third dialogue: how should a breach of school rules be dealt with?
Collecting and choosing examples
This group was very small, consisting of only four students aged eleven to thirteen and, unusually, the group decided to work with three examples. These were written up as follows (all names are fictitious):

Example 1
A boy, Chris, behaved badly in class. Several boys were talking and Chris could be heard above others. The teacher told Chris to leave the class, as it is against the school rules to talk when the teacher is speaking. Chris was picked out by the teacher but did not know what he'd done wrong. The teacher would not tell him. Instead Chris was told to go out of the room. The teacher and Chris got wound up and Chris was sent to the referral room.

Example 2
We were waiting outside. The teacher arrived, unlocked the room and we went to sit at our tables. The teacher started the lesson, when about six students came in laughing loudly. A table and some chairs were knocked down and one student, Rick, got knocked on the back of his head. Rick started laughing. The teacher got annoyed and sent Rick out. At the end of the lesson the teacher fetched Rick in, gave him 45 minutes detention, and would not listen to Rick, who wanted to explain.

Example 3
Jim did not have the right kit for PE. He wanted to explain, but the teacher gave him a detention. As it was the first lesson of the day it would have been difficult for Jim to explain in advance of the lesson.

Working with the chosen examples
After discussion, this group listed their judgements about the above examples as follows:

Example 1
- Had the teacher told Chris what was wrong in his action, the situation would have been diffused
- If Chris had been told what he'd done wrong, he'd have known what shouldn't be done in class

Example 2
- If the teacher had listened to Rick, the teacher's action might have been fairer

Example 3
- If the teacher had allowed Jim to explain, Jim might not have been in trouble

In reviewing their judgements, the group noticed that whereas examples one and two involved several students, example three involved only one. Noting this difference, they decided to identify what their examples and judgements had in common:

- A rule was broken
- There was lack of communication between teacher and student, no dialogue, no listening by the staff
- The way the breach of rule was dealt with was unfair
- Where more than one student was involved only one student's behaviour was dealt with – the student reprimanded was known for bad behaviour

A clear feeling emerged that the way breaches had been dealt with by the teachers was unfair, so the next question this group asked was 'Why was the teacher's action considered unfair?' Reasons were listed for Example 1, and then tested against the other two examples.

Why unfair in Example 1?
- Several students were involved, only one was disciplined
- The form of discipline was too harsh – instead a warning should have been given first
- The teacher did not justify or explain the measure taken (use of referral room)
- The student, Chris, was denied the opportunity to explain his action

In Example 2, the students thought the same reasons applied, except for the third one which was not applicable. In Example 3, the students thought the second and fourth reasons applied.

Reaching consensus
Having judged and analysed the three experiences in the above way, the students felt ready to leave aside their particular examples and return to the original question in more general terms. The following normative statements were agreed:

- A breach of rule *should* be dealt with by listening to both sides – student(s) and teacher

- The measure of discipline *should* depend on the seriousness of the breach

- Depending on the seriousness of the breach, teacher and student(s) *should* write a short report as soon as possible to avoid later dispute (each teacher *should* have an incident book).

The fourth dialogue: how should a breach of school rules be dealt with?
Collecting and choosing examples
This group was made up of ten students, aged eleven to fourteen, drawn from two schools in Greenwich. They decided to work with two of the listed examples (names are fictitious):

Example 1
Jodie and three friends were in the toilet area, truanting from a double information technology lesson. They made big tissue balls and threw them at the ceiling. The cleaner caught them and reported them to a senior member of staff. They were made to pick up all the cigarette butts off the toilet floor, and had a lunchtime detention. Their parents were not informed.

Example 2
Sarah and friends were on a residential visit with the school. They were smoking in the dormitory and set off the smoke alarm and the fire brigade came. Sarah and friends were not allowed to do any more activities for the rest of the trip and were excluded from school for three days. They were also barred from any further trips.

Working with the chosen examples
After exchanging their views about the examples, they listed the following judgements and reasons:

Example 1
- The parents of the truanting students should have been informed. All agreed with this view. The reasons given were that parents are informed about lesser breaches of rules. In this case a dialogue between parents and students about the reasons for truanting could have taken place. Furthermore,

parents could have taken their own sanctions (for example, stopped pocket money)

- Consensus was also reached about the measures taken: they were not severe enough for truanting from a lesson. Students suggested three alternatives: after school detention; going on report; community service

- Lastly, the group agreed that requiring the students to pick up cigarette butts was an inappropriate measure – without proper equipment this was unhygienic

Example 2
- There was consensus that 'no more activities' was an appropriate punishment, as was the three day exclusion, since it was a serious matter that the fire brigade was called out and their time wasted

- However, the students thought that 'no more trips' was too severe a sanction unless there is a review; after all, the students might be trustworthy in future

Reaching consensus
In this group, as in the third dialogue, the agreed answers were four 'should' statements:

- Measures against a breach of rules *should* be graded according to the seriousness of the offence and its consequences

- The first offence *should* be punished less severely than the second, third and so on

- The people who cause problems *should* take the blame and the action taken should be against them, not against the whole class

- The method of investigation *should* be such that students feel free to say what they want to say without being identified, especially in serious cases

The fifth dialogue: how should a breach of school rules be dealt with?
Collecting and choosing examples
The ten girls and boys who participated in this last of the Greenwich dialogues were all aged twelve to thirteen, from the same

class in the same school. On this occasion also two examples were chosen from those available (names are fictitious):

Example 1
There was a rule that we were not allowed to play 'torture run outs' because it is violent. There was a boys' and a girls' team; the boys had a letter (in their mind) and the girls had to beat them up until they discovered the letter – the teams took turns at this. The game was played although it was not allowed. After an accident free year playing this game, a boy was badly hurt by Sophie; the game had gone wrong and the injury was an accident. No action was taken against Sophie. For about two months the rule banning the game was strictly enforced and the game was not played. Then the pupils resumed playing the game, but teams were now mixed. On the second day two pupils got hurt – Tom had beaten up Katie and Stuart and was excluded for two days. After that the pupils decided not to play this game any more.

Example 2
Jasmine stole a lot of the spare exercise books from the classroom. So that she wouldn't get caught she hid some of them in the bags of two or three friends. She did this several times. After a month of stealing exercise books from the classroom the teacher noticed the stock was low and asked the class if they had anything to do with it. The teacher said that if no one owned up she would give a class detention; meanwhile the pupils had the opportunity to come up to the teacher during the lesson to tell her privately who it was. Two of the friends who had the books went to the teacher together and told her it was Jasmine. The teacher examined Jasmine's bag and took her to see the headteacher after school. Jasmine said she'd sold the exercise books, and she was excluded for two days.

Working with the chosen examples
In both examples exclusion had been used as the measure of sanction. Students questioned the appropriateness of exclusion and gave reasons for and against. These were the reasons given:

Example 1
In Example 1 most of the reasons given were against exclusion, with only one in favour.

- Exclusion is like a day off from working at school
- It was unfair towards Tom because Sophie hadn't been excluded for causing a more serious injury, even though both were accidents; thus there was unequal treatment between girls and boys
- Exclusion was too tough a measure
- Only one pupil was excluded instead of the whole group
- The one reason given in favour of the measure of exclusion was that it was appropriate because the headteacher may have wanted to control the level of violence in the school

Example 2
Contrasting views were put forward in the group about whether the exclusion in Example 2 was or was not an appropriate measure.

It was not appropriate because:

- It was too harsh for the action
- It was a fun day off school, instead of working
- It did not repair the damage
- The books should have been locked away

Exclusion was appropriate because:

- It would teach Jasmine not to do it again
- The books she had stolen are expensive and of value to the school and pupils
- Jasmine implicated other pupils
- Selling stolen goods is illegal

Reaching consensus
The agreed views collected together by the group at the end were:

- Internal exclusion is better than external exclusion because student learning continues under special supervision
- Individuals *should* not be singled out when the breach of rules is by a group – because of equality of treatment
- The measures taken *should* be tailored to the severity of the offence

Evaluation by students of dialogues 3, 4 and 5
On each of the three days in Greenwich the students gave their views of how they assessed the Socratic Dialogue they had experienced. In summary, the following points were made:

- Meeting and discussing with students from other schools was appreciated
- We learnt about being with and working with people we did not know before
- Having to keep to the point within a tight structure was valuable; it could help with other activities like essay writing
- Recording points on the flipchart was helpful but time-consuming
- We became more aware of the need for punishment
- It was good to have the opportunity to speak in a small group
- Working with different teachers built confidence
- To see the teachers' point of view was interesting
- It was hard to engage in one concentrated activity all day
- We saw links to citizenship in the curriculum

Evaluation by facilitator of Dialogues 3, 4 and 5
The Greenwich inter-borough experiment of running Socratic Dialogues for different groups over three successive weeks was worthwhile and showed that such initiatives can be successfully implemented by a teacher appointed to coordinate extra-curricular activities between different schools. The most difficult dialogue for the facilitator was the fifth, because the cross-fertilisation between age groups and schools was missing. However, this group, like the others, worked hard to reach some general conclusions.

In conclusion, it is worth noting that the students, in exploring their examples, discovered both *agreements* and *disagreements* over the measures the school had taken. This led to the formulation and recording of reasons in support of or against particular sanctions used in cases of a breach of school rules. The reasons given often illustrated student views on three issues:

- Fairness as between students involved in similar breaches of rules

- The appropriateness of the measure(s) taken against 'bad' behaviour: sanctions were often seen as too harsh or too soft for the given incident

- The lack of communication between staff and badly behaved students and between staff and parents

9

'WE HAD TO THINK FOR OURSELVES'

USING SOCRATIC DIALOGUE IN MATHEMATICS LESSONS IN A SECONDARY SCHOOL

Mechthild Goldstein

This account of Mechthild Goldstein's use of Socratic Dialogue in mathematics lessons with fifteen to sixteen year olds shows that Socratic Dialogue is well suited to developing the students' logical and mathematical thinking.

Beginning with fifteen-year-old students, mathematics is taught in streamed classes at our secondary modern school. As a rule, the mathematical knowledge taught in the basic course is only elementary. The extended course, by contrast, enables the students who are somewhat more proficient in mathematics to involve themselves more intensively with matters that, at least partially, go beyond the fundamental requirements.

I was teaching mathematics to fifteen and sixteen year old students, some of whom came from countries other than Germany. In each of two basic courses I ran a module on a geometrical topic, where I tried to shape the teaching along the lines of the Socratic Method. I will explain this 'Socratic experiment' in greater detail by the example of this module. An assistant who made video records and then transcribed excerpts of them attended these lessons. After the sequence of lessons he conducted short interviews with a few students. The quoted remarks by the students come from his transcript and from my personal notes.

The basic course in mathematics was attended by fifteen students (eight girls and seven boys). As this was a module within the framework of the regular mathematics lessons, the students were obliged to take part. However, students in the group had different degrees of motivation. Most had problems expressing themselves in such a way that the others could follow their train of thought. The Socratic Method, however, compels the group of participants to stay with an idea, to explain it in different ways, by different persons, until all have understood it. This, I found, was good practice for my group. Some of the students had considerable difficulties with the German language, which meant that they had even greater difficulties with active participation in a dialogue about a mathematical subject.

The module consisted of six working units, each corresponding to a 45-minute lesson within the regular timetable; these dialogue periods were spread over ten days. This caused some difficulties for a Socratic Dialogue: the gap between each lesson was rather long; in between them other subjects had been taught in line with the timetable. It also happened that two students were absent for a day or several days so missed at least one lesson of our module. I tried to meet this difficulty by ensuring that a brief summary of the progress of the process and a summary of the actual content of the dialogue so far were shared at the beginning of every lesson. By doing this, I hoped that everyone would begin each session on an equal footing.

In my introduction to the sequence of lessons I did not give a detailed exposition of the rules of the dialogue. I merely pointed out that this was an experiment that depended on the student group arriving jointly, and as far as possible independently, at the solution of a mathematical problem. I also emphasised the importance of reciprocal understanding, of listening and responding to one another, as well as the changed role of the teacher. Unlike regular lessons the teacher, as facilitator of the dialogue, would not make any substantive observations on content and would avoid assessments such as 'correct' or 'wrong'. Many contributions to the dialogue, as well as illustrations drawn by the students, were recorded on large posters to make sure they were not wiped away.

This ensured that they could be displayed in later lessons, making it possible to recreate the flow of the dialogue by consulting these written records.

The topic was: 'Can the radius of a circle always be projected exactly six times on the circle's circumference?' This fitted into the geometry curriculum for this age group both before the dialogue and later. (The mathematical background is the construction of a regular hexagon.) But the students were not given the question. They had to discover it for themselves.

In the first lesson I began by asking the students each to draw a circle for her or himself; next, to choose any point on the circumference and, from that point, to project the radius on the circumference several times, each intersection forming the starting point for the next projection. I had still not announced the actual question; the students themselves, and independently, discovered the phenomenon to be explained and made the question their own. At my suggestion they each produced a compass construction on paper. Predictably, their imprecise drawings gave rise to divergent results, which made a further, more accurate examination of the question a necessity for the students. Some students discovered very quickly: 'It comes out accurately'; 'It works six times'. Others found the sixth intersection point on the circumference to be before the starting point, and still others behind the starting point. Since I was not prepared to agree with any one group and declare their result correct, the need arose for closer investigation of the matter. Accordingly the students formulated the question: 'Can the radius of a circle always be projected exactly six times on its circumference?'

By now the students were quite motivated and most engaged keenly in the work. They had a multitude of creative ideas and initially tested a number of variants. For instance, they asked whether the radius could be projected more often on a larger circle than on a small one. However, following a number of drawings in their copybooks they decided not to pursue this question for the moment; they suspected that 'it always works six times' and wished to find a general justification for this. They therefore constructed a circle on a poster and in that circle drew various connecting lines (the circumferential points with each other and each with the central point). In this way a hexagon came into being, subdivided into six equilateral triangles. However, it took the participants a while before they realised that the triangles were equilateral and found a justification for it. They recognised certain lines and their function as they were repeated within the figure. ('We are drawing the diameter – it is a mirror axis'.) Moreover, they drew additional – more or less helpful – lines. It was particularly fascinating to observe how in this manner they recognised a multitude of other geometrical shapes within that one shape, and discussed their properties among themselves (rectangles, parallelograms, trapeziums) – properties which, in their previous lessons, had sometimes caused them great problems

After one student had suggested an examination of the angles in the (equilateral) triangles, the participants tried first to measure them – which I permitted. However, they soon discovered that this was an inaccurate method 'because nearly everybody gets different values'. Eventually a girl student remembered the axiom of the sum of the angles in a triangle; the students thereupon elucidated it one to another in a manner comprehensible to all. Finally, by united efforts, they found, on the basis of their previous knowledge, a solution that satisfied everybody – a consensus: 'The triangles have 60° angles. If six triangles are placed together at one corner (the origin), we get 360° (6 x 60°). Hence only exactly six triangles can fit in, no more and no fewer.' The individual elements in this chain of justification had been discovered step by step in the dialogue process and had been made comprehensible to everyone.

Admittedly, there were also frequent disturbances in the course of the lessons, such as flagging concentration and diminished motivation, that interrupted the dialogue and required intervention by the teacher. Again and again, the dialogue fluctuated between 'Socratic' and 'questioning' phases. Particularly striking was the difference in the behaviour of the participants – and of the teacher – during the different phases. During the Socratic Dialogue phases the students themselves assumed responsibility for the dialogue. They developed their own thread of ideas, listened and responded to one another. In short, they talked to one another and jointly developed a solution strategy. In the more questioning phases, familiar to them from their regular lessons, they relapsed into their usual behaviour in class. They did not communicate with one another, frequently sought the teacher's confirmation of what they were saying and so surrendered much of their responsibility to the facilitator. I too relapsed repeatedly into the usual teacher role. However, I did manage to restrain myself in matters of content and did not manipulate the course of the conversation about content. One student expressed this as follows: 'Frau Goldstein didn't help us at all. We had to tackle it ourselves, to see whether we got anywhere'.

The Socratic phases of the topic made a deeper impression on the students than the other phases. One girl said afterwards that she had somehow felt 'responsible': 'I had both to speak my own mind and always listen to the others ...'.

All the students took an active part in the dialogue. One girl said: 'It was always interesting, because each time different students said something (...) and that made it even more interesting. And then we could always express our own view, whether we thought it correct or not.' It was especially striking that students who had been poor performers in mathematics until then co-operated keenly and occasionally even advanced the dialogue significantly. One of the weaker students in particular was evidently fascinated by the mathematical point under discussion. He concerned himself with the questions raised in class during his free time and even approached me with it during lunch. It was he who eventually contributed the fruitful idea of conducting the proof by considering the 60° angles in the equilateral triangle. No doubt this had been a profound experience for this student: he, who normally could not sparkle in his mathematical performance had such a good idea that he brought the entire group significantly closer to the solution of a mathematical problem. Afterwards he remarked: 'That was really interesting. That one of us actually had the idea. And this time most of us were able to put our hands up and prove that we knew something, showing that 'yes, I really do understand it'. And demonstrated it'.

At the end of the dialogue unit of six lessons there was only a short meta-dialogue. In it, and in subsequent individual interviews, the students voiced the impression that they had found the solution to the problem 'all by themselves', without help from the teacher. 'We had to think for ourselves', one student remarked, visibly surprised and pleased. Besides, they had had more time for reflection than in normal class work. '... Frau Goldstein left us time to reflect. There was no hurry. We had lots of time to reflect on what we would discover'; 'So we took time over it. I think that's better than a hectic atmosphere'.

Comment

In view of the plentiful subject matter to be mastered during a semester it might seem extravagant to devote six lessons to a seemingly commonplace and trivial mathematical matter. But in the course of working on their (self-chosen) question the student group touched on further mathematical areas, gaining insights that until then had been unclear to them (eg in the above-mentioned context of different geometrical shapes).

I also believe that one should not underestimate the often much greater motivation and the working atmosphere that prevailed during the Socratic phases. All the students reported that they had experienced very positively the features and rules of the Socratic Dialogue they encountered during the six lessons. The atmosphere during the dialogue had been better than usual, and the group had co-operated far better. One student said: 'We also helped one another. This means that we participated as a community instead of as now, each one for himself'. Another said: 'We did it that time in group communities, not always individually. And that was better than if we had worked individually. Yes, we learnt to work together in groups. Everyone had to listen to the others'. Asked whether he thought this had actually worked, he replied: 'Yes, it worked. Perhaps it will now also function during class work.'

I too found this 'Socratic experiment' a very positive experience. I believe that, in spite of certain unfavourable school conditions, essential elements of a Socratic Dialogue emerged and produced entirely positive results – as proved by the feedback from the students. I have decided, not least in response to the students' wishes, to follow up this experience and plan more such experiments. I later had the impression that, as a result of their involvement, this group of students had made considerable strides, not only in their personal development and as a group, but also in their understanding of mathematical material. In later lessons, it became apparent that they really understood certain mathematical concepts, like the sum of the angles of a triangle or the features of an equilateral triangle, as they had registered the mathematical principles.

Through Socratic Dialogue, these students probably had an experience that strengthened their self-confidence, as shown by the comment of one student from the basic course: 'We can achieve something after all'. I think this was a remarkable statement, given it was made by a student from a group which is often seen as failing in mathematics. And the same student added: 'We actually solved all that. I think we had a lot of fun'.

10

SOCRATIC DIALOGUE IN PHILOSOPHY TEACHING IN THE SIXTH FORM

Barbara Neisser

Barbara Neisser describes two examples of using Socratic Dialogue in philosophy lessons with young people aged seventeen to twenty. She outlines the organisational conditions within which she worked in Germany, the process of the dialogue and its results. She reflects on and evaluates the teaching-learning process from her own perspective.

Preliminary note

Philosophy is a compulsory subject in the upper sixth form of grammar schools for all students who do not take part in religious instruction. Philosophy is moreover an optional examined subject in the sixth form. My chapter refers solely to the basic courses of philosophy for philosophy students aged sixteen to twenty.

I propose to structure my observations into four points:

- Why should Socratic Dialogue as a method of philosophising be integrated into the curriculum of the sixth form?
- What are the prerequisites of successful Socratic philosophy teaching?
- A report on two examples from practice
- Conclusions from practical experience

Why should Socratic Dialogue be integrated into philosophy teaching?

Philosophy teaching in the sixth form presupposes an understanding of philosophy that, on the one hand, links up with the critical philosophy of the Enlightenment and, on the other, sees itself as philosophy of dialogue, as a process of philosophising:

> Philosophy asks methodically about the general foundations of our assumptions of reality and our orientations towards life and action ... about people's insights into the human self, and their social and political systems, about the criteria of truth and the validity of norms.
>
> Philosophy critically examines the claims to validity of assumptions of reality and orientations towards life and action, as well as the legitimacy of social, political and legal orders. (*Guidelines for the Subject Philosophy*, North Rhine Westphalia – *Richtlinien für das Fach Philosophie*, NRW, p26).

Philosophy is understood, as it is in Socratic Dialogue, as regressive and critical analysis. Questions are to be asked about fundamental principles but there is also critical reflection on the existing claims to validity.

In the spirit of this critical, discursive understanding of philosophy, the individual disciplines of philosophy – anthropology, ethics, political philosophy, theory of knowledge, theory of science, philosophy of history, aesthetics and/or metaphysics – are thematised with the help of concrete questions. Philosophical discourse within the curriculum cannot presuppose any systematic or historical knowledge of philosophy. It must proceed from philosophical questions stemming from the practical experience of young people and from their everyday understanding.

Parallel to covering the substance of topic areas, philosophy teaching of the age group sixteen to twenty should transmit to students a series of methodical skills without which they would be unable to conduct a systematic reflective discourse.

A few of these skills are to be able, as an individual:

- to examine rigorously the links in philosophical and non-philosophical argument and reflect on them as to their correctness

- to question scientific and non-scientific interpretations as to their premises, consequences and potential epistemological interest
- to be able to express concepts with precision, and to use language correctly and consistently
- to be able to engage in rational and argumentative discussion with a dialogue partner
- to perceive the potential for and limits to independent and creative thought
- to know the difference between a discussion and an argument

The purpose of philosophy teaching is to provide students with skills for the analysis of arguments, to enhance their capacity for argument and for conveying independent critical questions and judgements. These competences lie not merely at cognitive level; they have only partially been practised in other school subjects and therefore cannot be taken for granted. In particular, critical insight into the questionable and provisional nature of their own points of view and of individual claims to validity is often, for a variety of reasons, difficult to achieve in this stage of transition from puberty to adulthood.

Socratic Dialogue is well suited both in structure and in the understanding of the self to develop the philosophical insights that underpin all philosophy lessons. From this point of view, Socratic Dialogue might be seen as the optimal method of philosophy learning in the upper school. Through it, the autonomous thinking, rational reflection and argumentative skills of students could be enhanced in their totality. In particular, the meta-dialogue can make a major contribution to a factual assessment and self-appraisal of a student's own learning and behaviour processes.

If, however, we consider the persons involved in this process of teaching and learning, the learning targets and the institutional conditions of the learning process at school, we quickly realise that philosophy learning cannot in the long run be achieved exclusively in the form of Socratic seminars. For one thing, lessons are also supposed to transmit knowledge of problems and interpretations of philosophical texts as well as knowledge of the history of philosophy. For another, the continual compulsion to engage in reflection, in regressive abstraction and in argument would, over a period of three years, overtax the young people and their teachers.

In addition, there is a whole string of external conditions and structural features of the learning process in schools that places considerable obstacles in the way of the Socratic teaching of philosophy. For example:

- The customary 45-minute rhythm of lessons
- The size of the class (mostly more than fifteen students)
- The traditional teacher-student relationship: the teacher as planner and shaper of the teaching process, with students as the recipients and consumers of lessons
- Awarding of grades
- The volume of subject-matter to be covered
- Lack of discipline, concentration and the absence of skills in argument in some student groups

Even though the regular learning of philosophy by the Socratic Method does not seem practicable in the upper school, I nevertheless consider it meaningful and desirable for Socratic phases – that is, periodic lessons in the form of Socratic Dialogue – to be introduced into philosophy lessons.

My reasons for such an integration of Socratic Dialogue are not only the underlying understanding it gives of philosophy, but also the requirement that a variety of teaching methods be used in lessons. Alongside the analysis of texts providing historical knowledge and an awareness of problems, teaching phases oriented towards dialogue provide an opportunity for analysing and reflecting on complex situations and personal experience. Reasons can be formulated in a generally comprehensible way and one learns to argue and come to terms with a subject and with people who think differently. Teachers influenced by a Socratic approach should also introduce project learning and phases of inter-disciplinary teaching into philosophy lessons.

More than any other teaching method, Socratic Dialogue offers the opportunity for an intensive and all-embracing practice of critical reflective dialogue and of autonomous rational thinking in an inter-disciplinary sense.

What are the prerequisites of successful Socratic philosophy teaching?

Socratic Dialogue in the Nelson and Heckmann tradition is a joint quest for true insights and reasoned conversation in groups (of about eight to fifteen people). It presupposes certain organisational conditions that are not always present in learning arrangements in schools. The following organisational and student-group-specific prerequisites are therefore crucial to the success of Socratic teaching. Particular attention should be given to ensure:

- that philosophy is not taught in single periods (45 minutes). A double-length lesson or even a three-period block per week is the indispensable time prerequisite for a Socratic seminar in school. Thematic or project weeks are especially suitable for Socratic teaching

- that there are no more than fifteen students in a philosophy class

- that teaching by the Socratic Method extends over no more than four or five weeks. More prolonged Socratic Dialogues overtax the students and are difficult to integrate into the structure of the upper school programme because of written examinations and quarterly grades, among other reasons

- that a written report is prepared of every Socratic seminar. This can be produced either by an individual student or by all the students in the class. It is important that this record is presented at the beginning of the next Socratic session and that students and teacher go through it and together find their entry into the subject and the dialogue process. The teacher should make a report of the entire development of the dialogue, independently of the records made by the students

- that the rules of the Socratic Dialogue, the special role of the teacher as facilitator, the demands on the participants, the special features of the meta-dialogue are all conveyed to the students before the beginning of the dialogue. They themselves should decide whether they want to participate in such a seminar and whether they can accept the rules of the dialogue as binding

- that the students clearly realise their obligation to observe the rules consistently as a necessary and constituent element of the joint reflection process

- that even prior to the Socratic teaching-learning process the teacher-student relationship is such that the students at times participate in the planning of the subjects taught

- that there are no students with behavioural problems in the learning group; that the learning group has no obvious problems with discipline

A difficult problem is the assessment of student work in the Socratic Dialogue. I would plead for a total suspension of grade-giving during the Socratic phase or, if that is impossible, to base marking solely on the written reports of the seminars.

It is useful, by way of preparation, for students to gain some initiation into philosophical topics (such as the significance of Kant's fundamental questions), into systematic argument and into the analysis of questions and communicative processes.

Introductory exercises in logic or the reading of extracts from a Platonic dialogue, and the discussion of the Socrates of antiquity (as the archetype of a reflective thinker) can also be good preparations for Socratic teaching.

Experience of Socratic Dialogues in philosophy teaching

My own experience of Socratic Dialogue has been gained over the past few years in philosophy teaching at basic level. Seminars are held one period a week over three consecutive weeks. The students are accustomed to working independently in groups and on projects. Teacher-student relations in the upper school are characterised by personal communication beyond what occurs in class during subject lessons. Teachers and students work as a team; the students have been accustomed to group and team work since the lower sixth.

I present here two cases of experience with Socratic Dialogue with the sixth form. Both Socratic Dialogues took place during the half-year when the theme was 'Ethics'; they involve a topical ethical problem chosen by the students themselves.

The first Socratic Dialogue
First phase: introduction

Organisation of the teaching/learning process: The philosophy class consisted of sixteen students, of whom twelve or thirteen took an active part throughout and were absent only in exceptional circumstances.

Previously covered lesson content was: concept of ethics, ethical norms, differentiation from other norms, and different philosophical reasons for ethical norms.

Dialogue question: 'Under what conditions should assisted dying be ethically permitted?'

Point of entry and first phase: formulation of the subject and definition of framework conditions. Within the context of addressing topical ethical problems the students chose their subject for the Socratic Dialogue from a list of five or six themes.

Search for examples: All students were given the task of thinking over an example from their own range of experience by the following week.

Arrangements for written reports: All students clearly recognised that a written record must always be kept. We agreed that turns would be taken by students in alphabetical order of their names. Two students had always to write an 'official report' and present it the following week. All were to take their own notes and copy the steps recorded on the blackboard. At the beginning of each weekly teaching block a *meta-dialogue* was held about the dialogue so far, starting from the relevant written records. As a rule the meta-dialogue was brief – about ten to fifteen minutes.

Limitation: We limited the Socratic seminar phase to four weeks; after that the dialogue was to be discontinued. In fact we eventually used a fifth teaching block to arrive at a general answer to our initial question and to conduct a concluding meta-dialogue.

Second phase: choice of the example (one block)

Not all the students had thought of a suitable example. From the examples put forward, one from a boy's own family immediately offered itself. He presented it in detail as a topical family problem.

The problem of assisted dying arose in this example only indirectly. His grandparents were caring for an aunt aged 105, who was bedridden and confused. The intensive care given to the aunt was overtaxing the grandparents, whose own health suffered. Consequently, their children and grandchildren wanted to place the aunt in a nursing home. This, in the opinion of all members of the family, would cause her to die soon.

I had serious misgivings about this example. In my judgement the conflict was too topical, the author of the example too involved emotionally, and the subject of the dialogue was addressed only indirectly. All the students, however, pleaded in favour of it. I explained my misgivings and asked the provider of the example about his knowledge, its separate aspects, and about his potential emotional problems. He himself wished the example to be discussed because he could see no ethically justified answer to his family's problem. His grandparents opposed the transfer of the old aunt to a nursing home, but he did not understand their attitude.

We chose his example and in retrospect it proved to be a piece of good luck. The provider was constantly ready with information, he brought his emotions into the argument and throughout the time of our dialogue he conducted a parallel discussion at home with his mother.

Third phase: analysis of the example (two to three blocks)
The students set about analysing the example with great seriousness. The old aunt's state of health, the physical and mental condition of the caring grandparents, the interests and situation of the children, Timo's (the example giver) own views and interests were examined and analysed.

In this phase I had little cause to intervene in order to steer the dialogue. Sometimes several points were addressed simultaneously and we had to agree on the sequence and on the importance of particular aspects for our subject.

Fourth phase: regressive abstraction (one to two blocks)
From analysis of the example it was difficult to develop criteria for judging the conditions under which assisted dying was permissible or should be provided. In contrast to Timo's family, it was by no means clear to the students in the seminar that placing the old aunt in a nursing home should be equated with an act of assisted dying. The question was asked, 'What made life worth living?' Time and again accounts of the interests and life situation of the people involved in the example were repeated.

I intervened several times to clarify the level on which our dialogue found itself. Portrayal of the values and standards by which the caring grandparents had lived all their lives eventually enabled us to make progress in the dialogue. It became clear that placing the old aunt in a nursing home ran counter to the ethical principles and norms of the grandparents and would go against their value concepts of humanity, family ties and obligations. Moreover, the answer to the question as to whether the old aunt's life was still worth living produced this result: if any assistance in dying, albeit in this case an indirect one, offended against the conviction and will of the aunt and of the grandparents then, from an ethical point of view, it could neither be demanded nor enforced by the rest of the family. Holding on to their own ethical convictions was the reason why the grandparents had decided to care for the aunt until her death despite the burden this imposed on them. For a solution to their problem it was suggested that the family might resort to professional help from nursing staff in order to relieve the grandparents at times.

Fifth phase: generalisation (one teaching period)
This step was quickly accomplished. The generalised answer to our original question that we found by analysis of the example was: Assisted dying can be ethically permissible only with the consent of those involved (the dying person, his/her closest relatives). There is no universally valid, ethically correct position on this question; in each individual case it must always be posed anew.

Comment:
The students were exceedingly satisfied with their Socratic Dialogue. In the concluding meta-dialogue they assessed exact analysis and argument as an important learning process. The same class later conducted another Socratic Dialogue on the subject: 'What norms should be valid for the community in a multicultural society?' On this occasion we worked for a time in two groups on two different examples. One group of students worked without a facilitator. The phase of regressive abstraction did not come off so well, with the result that at the end of the dialogue we were unable to give generalised answers to our question.

The second Socratic Dialogue
The procedure used was the same as for the first example. The class consisted of fifteen students, of whom about ten were active; three students were frequently absent and two seldom or never participated in the dialogue seminar; one student of the ten active participants at times had considerable discipline problems.

In spite of these less than optimal conditions I wanted to conduct a Socratic phase with this group on the overarching subject 'Topical ethical problems'. The students chose the following subject:

Dialogue question: 'How is infidelity in a partnership to be assessed ethically?' The formulation of the question surprised me.

First phase: introduction
Arrangements for written reports: We omitted to agree in advance who, and in what order, would write the report, with the result that it took us a long time in each session to find a report-writer.

Limitations: We limited the time-span of the Socratic Dialogue to four weeks. Within those four weeks the teaching block was cancelled for one week.

Second phase: choice of the example
Three examples for the subject were presented in the seminar, none of which seemed to me suitable. One example concerned the life of the mother of one of the students and dated back some twenty years. Another concerned the relationship of a boy with his girl friend: the problem here was only of a fictitious infidelity. The third example concerned the ongoing adultery of a Turkish woman in a village in Anatolia and was proposed by a Turkish girl student.

In the absence of a truly suitable example I should really have put an end to the dialogue at once. However, I allowed myself to be persuaded by the students, who were by now very keen on this kind of lesson, and tried, after all, to use the example from the life of a student's mother. The student was given the task of exploring his incompletely presented example in full detail by the next lesson and then to re-present it. I had considerable doubts on this score – and the student withdrew his example the following week. We then considered the Turkish girl's example of adultery in the Anatolian village. She was able to provide all the details of the example. She was a conscientious, responsible student who argued rationally. So we attempted to work with this example. I put aside my misgivings that the different cultural ideas contained in that example of matrimonial and sexual morality might become an insuperable problem as we worked on it.

Third phase: analysis of the example

Even in the first phase the class had divided into three groups during the analysis of the example. On one side were Turkish and a few German girls, on the other a group of four boys; the rest scarcely participated (if at all) in the dialogue. The Turkish girls and the German boys fought each other over the question as to whether there was any infidelity at all in the example. The fact that the woman had been forced by her parents to marry a man she did not love was an argument, mainly for the boys, in favour of not judging her subsequent adultery as infidelity. The counter-argument that the woman had lived in a marriage with her husband over many years, had had children by him and that an intimate relationship of trust existed between her, her husband and her children, was not accepted. Owing to the difference of ideas on matrimonial morality no common view was attained in this example.

The boys, moreover, were unable to separate my function as facilitator from my role as teacher. Time and again during the content dialogue, they accused me of failing to express a view on the substance of the question and argued that I should ensure clarification of the issue.

I terminated the dialogue during the third phase. In a subsequent meta-dialogue I justified my decision, elucidated the problem with the example and explained why, in my opinion, we should never have used that example. Once more I dealt with the accusations about my facilitation of the dialogue and tried to explain the difference between my role as a teacher and that of Socratic facilitator, in which I was obliged to hold back on matters of content.

Comment

In retrospect I ask myself whether I had sufficiently and correctly assessed the group dynamics in this seminar before planning the Socratic phase.

The dialogue made me realise once more how important it is to have a really suitable example that is drawn from the experience of the students themselves.

In order to enable the students to reconnect with the overarching subject of ethics, they were to formulate a written answer to the question: 'How is infidelity in a partnership to be assessed ethically?' two weeks after the discontinuation of the dialogue. The written answers were subsequently presented by their authors. Nearly all the participants in the class arrived at the same conclusion, which may be summarised as follows:

Infidelity in a partnership should be regarded as unacceptable from an ethical point of view and must be judged as bad for human relations. In the case of infidelity one person's trust is invariably abused and destroyed. Such a breach of trust can have such negative consequences for some people that they can never again build up a solid relationship of trust with another person. Thus individual infidelity also damages society as a whole.

This answer, formulated by the students in their individual work, proved to me that in spite of the failed dialogue they had reflected on the problem and, by relating their reflections to the substance of their previous learning, had arrived at appropriate insights. What astonished me was their wish to conduct another Socratic Dialogue in class as soon as possible. They justified this wish as follows:

The dialogue had not led to an outcome, and had at times been 'confused and chaotic'. Even so, the students, through their own efforts to investigate the problem and find judgements on partial questions, had nevertheless learned more than had they read texts or discussed philosophical theses or theories expounded to them by a teacher.

In retrospect I consider the meta-dialogues during the Socratic phase to be of especial importance. The group of boys, who more or less dominated every class discussion, realised during the meta-dialogue that their seminar behaviour had disturbed other participants in their intensive reflection and systematic argument. They also realised that in a philosophical dialogue it is not important to prevail with one's own opinion at all costs, but rather to listen to the arguments of the other participants in the dialogue and to judge their correctness.

Conclusions from my practical experience
In addition to the examples of Socratic Dialogues presented here, which covered a prolonged period of time, I have conducted Socratically-influenced discussions of one to two teaching blocks

with different classes on a variety of topics. Through these I have experienced that the students' active participation and interest in philosophical questions can be greatly enhanced by dialogues which proceed from their own concrete experiences. In repeated meta-dialogues with student groups it became clear from their observations how they assessed our dialogues:

- The students are impressed by their experience of Socratic Dialogue

- Their attitude to the subject changes; their seriousness intensifies during systematically analysing themes and questions on their own

- For young people an important motivation for philosophising is to gain well-founded views on questions concerning their own lives and orientation. This can be met by Socratic Dialogue in class

- Without a genuinely suitable example Socratic Dialogue with adolescents is difficult. An example from their own range of experience is, in my opinion, indispensable

- A tense group-dynamic situation in class, or one determined by an overbearing opinion leader, is a poor or unsuitable starting point for a Socratic Dialogue

- The meta-dialogue offers a good opportunity for an exchange of views on the teaching process; for a rational discussion of disturbances and tensions, and for the common consideration of solutions. It can also be introduced into other subjects and learning processes of the upper school. It provides an opportunity for systematic practice of self-reflection, for discussion with students of questions of method and for relieving the teaching process of group-dynamics

PART III
Theory in relation to practice

11

THE SOCRATIC APPROACH AT SCHOOL LEVEL: FOUR MODELS

Gisela Raupach-Strey

The author conducted an extensive research study about Socratic Dialogue in the context of school and professional training in Germany. This text is taken from a section entitled *The positive potential of the Socratic Paradigm at school level: four models*. The use of the scientific concept 'paradigm' treats Socratic Dialogue at a theoretical level. It embraces all aims, procedures and rules of the dialogue and their validity. The editors have shortened the text and omitted all footnotes. Gisela Raupach-Strey has drawn on numerous articles about teaching and learning as well as on her own experience as a Socratic facilitator in schools, universities and other educational institutions in Germany. In this chapter she discusses how Socratic Dialogue, or elements of Socratic Dialogue, can be organised and practised within the framework of schools and presents four models illustrating how to achieve this.

Introduction

We can distinguish between four models for Socratic work in schools, taking account of the sometimes adverse conditions in schools:

Model 1
One-off Socratic Dialogues can take place within the framework of the school either in the time available during theme weeks for a limited period or during normal class work. Both these variants of Socratic work give the dialogue an unusual character.

Model 2
Elements of the Socratic Method, where considered fruitful, are singly integrated into the usual lessons.

Model 3
Teaching a subject is planned on Socratic lines overall: the theory and practice of the Socratic approach provides the basic orientation. Even in this case there is incomplete realisation of the approach. Instead, appropriate allowances are made to take account of the conditions in the school. A balance is struck between Socratic requirements and the indispensable 'non-Socratic' demands of an institutional nature (eg the award of grades) and of an educational and theoretical nature (eg the acquisition of certain areas of knowledge). This model, suitable for the teaching of philosophy, may also, by analogy, be seen as suitable for the teaching of ethics. The model is not equally suitable for all subjects.

Model 4
The practising teacher uses the Socratic approach as a supplementary tool, as a critical standard for improving and deepening the teaching of subjects other than philosophy, by reflecting on basic philosophical foundations.

Discussion of models
Model 1: complete Socratic Dialogue
A complete Socratic Dialogue can be conducted in school only in special circumstances. The best opportunity would be during a theme week or as a project, when sufficient time is available and there is no problem with continuity. It is important to clarify the requirement that all participants in the group must remain together for the whole of the agreed time. This model makes the pursuit of different objectives possible – either the method itself becomes known as it is practised or, where there is interest in a particular topic, the group can work on this with the aid of the Socratic Method. We can imagine a particular aspect of a subject

that can be worked on Socratically. This applies particularly to subjects that are new to all students, for example philosophy or ethics. Finally, within overarching themes like 'living differently', 'foreigners' or 'the future', the entire school might be shown what pure reflection within a dialogue group can contribute to a theme week.

If it is intended to integrate a Socratic Dialogue into normal class work, a certain period of time, possibly three weeks, may be assigned to it. It is advantageous to use double periods or to combine lessons in some other way. With this pattern difficulties can arise from the long breaks, possibly of several days, between lessons because participants are absent. On the other hand, such a dialogue can be a phase of concentrated teaching that is deliberately separated from other lessons using different methods. The unusual character of the dialogue method can be advantageous or disadvantageous, depending on the learning situation. Yet for once the goal of demonstrating the possible thoroughness of the intellectual process will almost certainly be attained without restriction.

This model has been repeatedly tested in practice by Socratic facilitators who are also teachers, in such diverse subjects as philosophy, mathematics, politics and physics, as well as in various age groups and school types [grammar, comprehensive and primary schools. Chapters 5, 8 and 9 in this book provide informative examples of such work. eds].

A striking feature of these experiments is that the students are profoundly aware of the difference in the roles of teacher and Socratic facilitator. The restraint practised by the teacher is unusual in the school context and requires some getting used to. Equally unusual is the potential and indeed expected independent activity by the students. This also needs getting used to – mainly by the students themselves though it can also surprise the teacher. Most emphasis is given to the improved atmosphere during the dialogue, and the direct contact with the subject matter.

In terms of content, the students are most aware of having discovered their own competence in a subject. For example, students discovered by themselves the idea of a 'great philosopher' or a whole range of perspectives on a subject in a way previously unsuspected.

The teachers themselves may have to become accustomed to a Socratic style of guidance, which is different from the usual style of guidance within the school framework. Anyone familiar with both roles and frequently practising them will occasionally have to remind themselves in which role they are acting at that moment. On the other hand, there is the question of whether the roles of the teacher and the Socratic facilitator should be separated so strictly in relation to the manner of steering the dialogue. This question arises again in Model 3.

Model 2: integration of single elements

What elements of the Socratic Method can possibly be integrated with other forms of teaching independently of a full dialogue process? Teachers in further education frequently notice such possibilities which are not limited to certain subjects. The following list contains some examples from the perspective of teachers of such methodological elements:

- Stimulating mental alertness and encouraging students to put their own questions

- Directing the student group to their own thinking: questions not answered by the teacher but passed on to the student group

- 'Midwifery skill': helping students articulate or more clearly formulate their own idea or opinion, even when they do not find this easy, and waiting patiently for their statements

- Establishing and consolidating mutual understanding: when an opinion has been expressed, ask the rest of the student group how it was understood

- Establishing a reference to experience and avoiding judgements of too general a nature by asking for examples to illustrate assertions made

- Taking assertions seriously without commenting on them and asking for the justification of assertions made; possibly continuing to ask for the reasons and for the justification

- Viewing assertions critically and structuring their justification: questioning the student group as to the persuasive power of the justification and possibly asking for further reasons

- Guiding thinking beyond familiar tracks: asking the student group for alternatives to a thesis or position; overcoming black-and-white thinking

- Taking the course of the discussion and one's own statements seriously and not asking a new question until the preceding one has been fully answered

- Tolerating silence

- Encouraging the adoption of (justified) positions, as well as mutual respect: formulating one's own thoughts, for example as an answer to a question, possibly recording it in writing and subsequently letting everyone read it aloud; listening to other opinions without prejudging them

- Making the group participate in steering the lesson: discussing with the student group the procedures used during lessons; the teacher temporarily surrendering the facilitating role

- Allowing oneself time.

Generally speaking, it should be possible to apply such elements of the method in normal class work separate from a Socratic Dialogue, even though their purpose (also in their interaction) will probably emerge more clearly when using a fully Socratic procedure. However, as additional elements in a repertoire of instrumental methods they could be liable to being misunderstood or even abused. Their effectiveness depends primarily on whether teachers apply them in a Socratic spirit, in which case they might prove useful to students. For teachers these Socratic elements are often the first steps to recognising and utilising the numerous opportunities of the Socratic approach.

Model 3: design of whole lessons
The third model, that of shaping classroom teaching entirely on the Socratic model, can work positively in the teaching of philosophy. There exist certain procedural differences between class discussion (even from a Socratic perspective) and Socratic Dialogue in its standard form. The teacher's awareness of these differences may help him or her to identify the method's benefits and limitations. To make this clear, the points below identify the strategies used by the teacher during lessons on the one hand, and by the Socratic facilitator on the other, although there is considerable overlap, particularly in Model 3:

- The teacher shows interest in almost every question raised by a student and indicates that in principle it merits discussion. But the teacher will *also* bear in mind that lessons are set within the institutional framework. This will influence the teacher's choice of problems and the detailed joint examination of related questions. Unless the group has already played its part in taking the decision, the teacher will make the decision clear to the group. Given a little flexibility and imagination, student questions can be accommodated more often than is sometimes assumed, although there will be exceptions

- In a Socratic Dialogue a *single* train of thought is developed in the group over a longer stretch of time. In classwork the trains of thought are not only shorter, but *breaks* often occur. Frequently the thread in the discussion has to be broken off for various reasons and it is often not possible to take it up again at the same point. In the light of the non-homogeneity of a larger student group it may even be advisable deliberately to break off a discussion and then to bring the group together again at a different point. Breaks in the sequence of a discussion, even when pragmatically useful or downright necessary are, from a Socratic perspective, something that just has to be accepted, in the hope that the context can later be re-established in another way

- The insights gained during lessons need not all emerge in *one* continuous phase of the discussion, but can also be arrived at step by step. Sometimes a new start is made without direct connection between one point and the next. In exceptional cases this can be made explicit by means of a list or a diagram, though care should be taken that these do not become *substitutes* for insights. Placing aspects of the subject or insights side by side or one after another is no more than a sequential arrangement. Implicit in this is the tacit anticipation of a synthesis reached individually or subsequently through group discussion

- Occasionally the teacher provides greater help in matters of substance in the dialogue than does the Socratic facilitator. The maieutic aspect of Socratic Dialogue is characterised by the greatest possible facilitator restraint, so that the participants may themselves discover insights. Along with giving students language help, the teacher will also make more references to the content. Such teacher-led interventions are best when drawing on earlier elements of the discussion rather than on the teacher's own knowledge. The aim here is to ease the establishment of connections or to give prominence to the most salient point. Moreover, in a larger group any maieutic one-to-one dialogues should, out of consideration for other students, occupy only brief phases

- In steering the dialogue the teacher is not as reticent in matters of method as the Socratic facilitator. S/he will, for instance, draw attention to alternatives, recommend or, at some difficult point, even determine a particular direction so as to avoid overburdening the learning group with decisions about the best way forward or other meta-reflections. In any case, the customary role expectation assigns to the teacher the task of structuring the work of the group. This expectation can only gradually be reduced. Nevertheless, the Socratic option is open to the teacher. The teacher can progressively share with the group the task of clarifying and making decisions about the course of discussion. By creating opportunities for students to assume responsibility for the course of the dialogue and its structure, a 'bird's eye view' can develop in the group. However, in less experienced groups, it may be good on pragmatic grounds for the teacher to shoulder responsibility for some of the difficulties

- The teacher gives more attention to the needs of a group made up of developing learners. Thus s/he will bring understanding to a situation where adolescence or earlier history impedes the patience span or the cognitive or communicative competence of the students. It may also mean that space is given for clarification of a particular question because, at that moment, it is charged with strong personal or emotional interest, even though the question is not all that relevant to the content dialogue

- Without altogether losing sight of it, the teacher initially puts aside the expectation of arriving at an outcome. The outcome of the dialogue should indeed be worked out by the learning group itself yet, as far as possible, it should *also* be compatible with certain expectations laid down in directives, course subject or examination constraints. This is by no means a case of squaring the circle; it need not be particularly difficult given the intrinsic logic of the subject

These seven points are not intended to lay down the norm for the way lessons should be conducted from a Socratic perspective. These reflections are based primarily on my long experience both as a teacher of philosophy in a school and as a Socratic facilitator of dialogue groups in a non-institutional setting, which allow me to make comparisons. It showed me that, *in certain circumstances*, it might be useful for lessons to deviate from the strict rules of Socratic Dialogue. This does not mean that demands are being set up for all classroom situations or that all seven points are invariably to be applied as a package. Deviations can in any case have different degrees and weightings, depending on the context. They are compatible with the maieutic principle provided they are not adopted in a patronising way. Potential departures from the stricter Socratic framework may be understood as forms of support for the learning groups concerned.

There is a certain asymmetry in the comparison between teacher and facilitator. In the classroom situation, allowance is made for actual conditions, whereas the Socratic Model tends to presuppose the 'ideal'. Yet in conducting Socratic Dialogues, the prevailing concrete conditions will also have to be considered and, according to the particular composition of the dialogue group, these considerations will have points in common with some school conditions. Even standard Socratic Dialogues have to work to a time limit. The necessary compromises can certainly help the group to achieve satisfactory progress in their discussion or even a satisfactory outcome. Moreover, one might question whether the principle of holding back in the role of the Socratic facilitator has perhaps been over-emphasised.

Model 4: evaluation of classroom practice
The Socratic approach can be a complementary and/or critical tool when used in the structuring of classroom activities. At the level of structure, the Socratic approach can provide a standard against which flaws in daily classroom communication and discussion of subject material can be measured against the possibility of something better. The experience of a German Socratic facilitator has shown that actual classroom practice can be noticeably affected by such assessments, even though the lesson is not there-

by transformed into a Socratic Dialogue. One of his girl students subsequently said, 'this is not how one usually speaks to one another, least of all at school'.

The available options in method largely correspond to those set out for Model 2. But here the purpose is different. In this model the Socratic approach operates as a regulatory idea. Overall the approach is assumed to be positive and desirable, and is accepted and used as a yardstick for assessing and shaping classroom communication. Implementation of this educationally more modest practice has been described by German facilitators as 'Socratically influenced communication'. The aim is that classroom discussion and the teaching-learning process should approximate to a Socratic Dialogue, but at the same time follow subject-specific objectives.

The Socratic paradigm in this context does not represent an overall plan for teaching the full spectrum of special subjects. This model is, however, suitable for such subjects as German language and literature or citizenship. Socratic Dialogue can help improve communication even in a difficult group. There is no need to delay its introduction until the prerequisites for discussion are met. There might be a risk that the Socratic approach be reduced to a mere tool for improving communication. This concern, however, is unnecessary so long as the Socratic attitude underpins all action and results in the acceptance of a critique of classroom behaviour. Model 4 shares with Model 3 the central importance of the Socratic attitude. An additional function of the Socratic approach can be to question the underlying principles of all subject specialisms. Equally relevant is the Socratic approach in interdisciplinary dialogue, required nowadays as well as in former times. For this reason, the relationship between the Socratic approach and school subjects will be explored.

School subjects and the Socratic approach

We have seen that the Socratic paradigm can be transferred and introduced into existing school conditions, using the four models outlined:

- Complete Socratic Dialogue
- Integration of single elements into lessons
- Design of whole lessons
- A standard in evaluation of classroom practice

Which of these models is the most suitable for a specific situation will depend, among other things, on the particular subject, especially on the content to be covered. In subjects involving the study of empirical data or which have empirical aspects – for example, natural sciences, history, sociology, psychology and religious studies – the conveying of information will inevitably play a major role during the early stages, just as the assimilation of knowledge will later on. Socratic Dialogue is unsuitable for both of these stages, which means that the Socratic Method can be considered only for other aspects of the work. For example, using the Socratic Method in the teaching of physics in school presupposes that students have sufficient prior knowledge (this refers to the state of knowledge at given ages in a particular subject). It is then possible to use Socratic ways of working to enable students to recognise unsolved problems. Students have to engage in some hard thinking and are then amazed at the new insights gained. In this way all subjects with empirical components can utilise Socratic ways of thinking, once the appropriate level of knowledge is attained.

Even in these subjects there are many learning processes for which the Socratic Method is useful. This applies initially to instances when questions arise about immediate personal experience in the lives of the students and where understanding is sought. Socratic procedures are especially suitable at the discovery stage, when students are independently seeking insights, when hypotheses are formulated and tested, or when criteria have to be clarified for the assessment and judgement of empirical data. Finally, the Socratic Method has its place in class work whenever questions of a fundamental nature are raised, for example, questions about the significance of the most basic elements of a subject. Questions such as: What is a physical, what is a historical event? Or questions seeking explanations of basic patterns such as: What is causality? What is a law? What is an intentional act? What does responsibility or humanity mean?

The situation is different in subjects that have the task of clarifying questions of validity (eg philosophy, ethics and mathematics). In these disciplines subject content does not consist of facts but of problems. Questions are raised about the foundations of human thought, action and being. In philosophy and ethics certain aspects of religious education might also come into this category, provided the teaching approach permits questions about its foundations. In mathematics it is questions about the validity of formal symbol relations or about problems of the relation between abstract subjects of geometry or number theory that can be considered. Model 3 offers itself: invariably questions of validity are examined and it is therefore possible to proceed by the Socratic Method, as it has the same purpose.

Mathematical laymen may be surprised to find the subject of mathematics included in this subject group. This may be because mathematics is frequently taught at school as knowledge of formulae and algorithms and their application, whereas the path to such knowledge is all too often neglected. Yet the educational value of this subject lies precisely in getting to know the typical subject-specific paths and their structural principles through a process of self-discovery. For many years I taught mathematics to grammar school students using a Socratic dialogue perspective, as far as possible to all age groups, in basic as well as advanced courses. The Socratic approach is not limited to certain age groups nor certain school types. This is clear from Mechthild Goldstein's chapter in this book about teaching mathematics in a secondary modern school. The Socratic Method has long been accepted in the teaching of mathematics in German schools.

Limitations on the applicability of Model 3 in this group of subjects are not of a fundamental but of a pragmatic nature. Account has to be taken of learning difficulties, of group dynamics, of existing levels of knowledge, understanding and, as mentioned earlier, of the institutional conditions found in schools. It is therefore no accident that representatives of the Socratic Method are to be found in lessons in this group of subjects, as they pose questions about validity and are concerned with problem solving. This does not rule out that *individual* Socratic elements can be tested. Teachers who as yet have little experience of the Socratic method may feel more secure with limited experiments. But the question is left open about the extent to which the purpose of the subject – clarification of validity questions – can be attained with non-Socratic methods. At least this is the question when class teaching is not understood purely in terms of the passing on of knowledge discovered by others, whether scientists or textbook authors.

Finally, the Socratic Method is particularly suited to interdisciplinary work, across the institutionalised division of subjects. This applies, for example, to general questions that concern people and that precede the content of school subjects. Under this heading come experiments with the Socratic Method in philosophy for children and in teaching philosophy in primary school, as illustrated in Ingrid Delgehausen's chapter in this book. Mention should also be made of ethics teaching at all ages. With older groups the Socratic approach can be used to deepen philosophical understanding of subjects and to explore questions which transcend subject boundaries or which identify links between subjects.

Subject boundaries

Reflection on the boundaries between subjects and how these can be transcended may be viewed from four perspectives.

1. *Questions about the foundations of the sciences which are included in the school curriculum*

In the first place the basic concepts which underpin the foundations of science need to be identified. Understandings gained through the Socratic approach of basic concepts, stemming from the everyday world outside school, can be meaningfully highlighted. They can be compared with scientific definitions – for example, the concept of 'force' in physics or the concept of 'duty' in Kant's philosophical theory. Furthermore, the methods and their effectiveness also belong to the foundations. Similarly general statements and assertions can be tested for validity, and the certainty of an insight can be checked by Socratic reflection. These elementary reflections can then be compared with the standardised methods of a science. Finally questions should be asked and Socratically examined about the fundamental concept of what one basically wishes to know in a natural science or in the humanities.

2. *Boundary problems between the sciences as well as between science and other areas like everyday life, technology, society, world views*

It is clearly impossible to prescribe the method of *one* science for the discussion of questions of boundary between the sciences. The openness of the Socratic Method is a positive recommendation in this respect. Examples may be drawn from medical ethics or from assessment of the consequences of technology. All key fundamental problems concerning the linking of subjects or the transcending of boundaries can be addressed Socratically. This is not to say, of course, that the Socratic Method is the only one by which these problems can be exhaustively dealt with; empirical methods and the Socratic approach can successfully complement one another. However, in the absence of Socratic philosophical questioning, the core problem in such interdisciplinary teaching may easily remain hidden. Thus the Socratic Method also serves the interdisciplinary approach that is nowadays demanded but not always realised.

3. *Critique of science*

The Socratic Method can also be applied to science as a whole. The immediacy of general, not yet specialised, questioning is important. On the one hand, questions should be asked about the purposes of scientific research; on the other, research should be assessed and eventually confronted with the assessments made by society. Socratic questioning is particularly suited to challenging unjustified beliefs in science and can raise the level of awareness about the way expertise is often overestimated.

4. *Ethics of science*

Under this heading questions may be raised about the applications of science, and about the ethics of science. Reflections about such questions should refer to fundamental ethical norms on the one hand and patterns of socio-political interest on the other.

Bringing to bear all four perspectives makes it possible, with support from the Socratic Method, to overcome an unreflected orientation towards science (scientism). Greater clarity is gained about the possibilities and limitations of science, about its purposes and possibly its attachment to special interests. Concentrated in the Socratic approach is the reasoning of laymen who, like jurors in court, provide a corrective in the fundamental socio-political questions of our scientific-technological world. In short, Socratic philosophising serves not only as an introduction to science but also as a critique of science in the broadest sense, as needed by a democratic public.

Summary

The Socratic approach is based on the principle that the arguments of all participants in the dialogue carry equal weight. Even if this is initially not possible between teachers and students, the presupposition is that potentially this will be the case.

In terms of organisational models, concepts and curriculum subjects, the positive features of using the Socratic approach may be summed up as follows:

- Students learn how to articulate their own questions and to ask genuine questions about a subject or problem

- Students have the opportunity to introduce their everyday experiences into class work and to penetrate them intellectually. The more abstract insights into their subject can be anchored in their experience and so better understood, provided they can be filled with imagination and illustrative material

- Students are able to discover that taking one's time and remaining calm are prerequisites of genuine and searching thought processes

- Verbal skills are enhanced by the requirement to formulate their own thoughts and arguments, as well as clarifying them

- Questions asked by dialogue participants as to whether they have correctly understood the ideas of others enhance mutual comprehension and communication among students

- Critical thinking develops skills in argument and awareness of problems

- Joint intellectual effort in the dialogue permits deeper penetration into the subject, fosters thoroughness and allows the emergence of genuine answers and insights to genuine questions

- Shaping and deciding on the course of the discussion enhances students' dialogue skills. With constant practice, self-confidence, the capacity to reason and the whole person are strengthened

- Overall, Socratic work in class promotes non-alienated (or less alienated) learning, at subjective, objective and inter-subjective levels.

12
SIX PEDAGOGICAL MEASURES AND SOCRATIC FACILITATION

Gustav Heckmann

This chapter is taken from two chapters in Gustav Heckmann's book *Socratic Dialogue*, first published in 1981. Heckmann developed the Socratic Method as a teaching-learning process and considered it as an opportunity for independent learning. In one chapter he described his seminar experiences with university students, using six pedagogical measures which he set out in his chapter. Also described are certain kinds of facilitator interventions which are calculated to steer the dialogue in fruitful directions and prevent it from running into the sand and getting no results. In the later parts of this chapter, the word 'intervention' is used to apply only to those interventions which lead the participants to pay attention to a question or aspect that derives from the main question. Thus participants have to decide whether they want to work with a question or to leave it aside. In good Socratic manner, Professor Heckmann started the section on Socratic facilitation by giving some examples of intervention in this narrow sense.

Before the Second World War, Heckmann had used Socratic Dialogue as a teacher in the boarding school founded by Nelson, first in Germany and then in Denmark and Britain. After 1945, he returned to Germany and became Professor of Education in Hannover. In working out his ideas, Heckmann built on Leonard Nelson's ideas (see chapter 13 on *The Socratic Method*) and on a text by Grete Henry-Hermann, Conquering Chance (see chapter 1).

Six pedagogical measures

It is a Socratic principle that insights into general relationships are won solely by means of the comprehension and analysis of concrete experience. In this process general knowledge can be articulated as it emerges from its close connection with concrete experience.

In a seminar about the topic 'the human will', we saw how Hans, in his battle for his identity, and particularly in overcoming a crushing defeat, was helped to overcome his fear by recognising the value of becoming 'the person he wanted to be'. With more time, we would surely have won the general insight, albeit further removed from the concrete, that recognition of a value enables someone to overcome an opposing force like fear.

In the seminar about mathematical truth we won insights into the structure of mathematical proof solely by working with the sentence about Pythagoras' Theorem and a few other sentences. By analysing the proofs that we ourselves discovered, we caught sight of the phenomenon of fundamental pre-conditions, and could then proceed to define the conceptual criteria.

Finally, in the seminar about freedom we reached insight into how Lore had to behave to gain more freedom. We did this solely by looking at the individual steps she took during the process of her emancipation. We recognised the significance of the individual steps, in particular the meaning of inner processes like Lore's openness to criticism, not brushing it aside, her recognition confirmed by her own feeling that the criticism contained an element of truth. Only by riveting our attention to each of these individual steps were we, and especially Lore herself, grasping their full meaning. Once we had recognised the importance of openness in Lore's achievement of greater freedom, we had taken the first step towards the general insight: for translating values into reality it is crucial when we act that we do not suppress fleeting awareness of our values and/or our conscience.

A dialogue is Socratic when it helps individual participants to gain general insights through reflection on concrete experience. The essential work this requires is outlined in the reports on our seminars. Only when the individual makes this effort will he [*sic*] gain insight. In the Socratic Dialogue, it is the facilitator's *pedagogical task* to ensure that this happens. What pedagogical measures are available for this?

Measure one: content impartiality

First and foremost, the facilitator has to nurture the participants' own capacity to judge by withholding his own opinion about the question being discussed. This requirement to hold back is certainly valid for the facilitator of Socratic Dialogues. As teacher he has to be ahead of his students in the topic under discussion and especially in the work required for gaining insights from experience. As a result his arguments, were he to express them, would carry more weight than those of the students, who would be disturbed in their uninhibited testing of their own arguments. Their alertness would be directed towards the facilitator's arguments and this would detract from their own thinking.

Nelson stressed that 'it is an indispensable requirement to prevent teacher judgements from exercising any influence. Where such influence is not excluded, all further effort is of no avail. The teacher will have done his best to steal a march over the student's own judgement by offering his own prejudice.'

Measure two: working from the concrete

The facilitator has to guide the participants to work from the concrete and to ensure that the link to the concrete is always in people's minds when they progress towards general insights. He will, for example, call on a participant to illustrate with an example a generally formulated thought. Examples in a Socratic Dialogue can be more or less suitable for this purpose. It is most fruitful to investigate one of the participants' real-life experiences, provided it can be presented openly and without embarrassment or shame. When it is not possible for the example-giver to communicate all relevant details, to the group the example cannot help the group illuminate the truth. But the facilitator should show patience if something speculative and artificially constructed is tabled first, rather than a real-life experience. In due course personal experiences will surely surface as the participants establish trust among each other.

Measure three: mutual understanding

The dialogue needs to be exhaustively exploited as an aid to thinking. The facilitator has to watch to see whether the participants really understand each other, and if in doubt try to foster such understanding. All participants have to make efforts in two directions: first, to express their own thoughts clearly so they can be understood by the others; second, to grasp the thoughts of others. The facilitator assists in both respects by asking 'How did you understand Paul?', and asking Paul, 'Have you been understood correctly?' Or if the facilitator has not yet understood a statement: 'I haven't yet grasped that point, can someone help me to understand what Grete means?' The participants' clarity and deepening of thought is nurtured by insisting on precise and shared understanding between them.

Measure four: focus on the current question

Whenever the dialogue digresses into adjacent questions, the facilitator has to bring the group's attention back to the unfinished point. He has to ensure that the group is aware which question is being discussed at that moment. He has to keep the group on track until this question is sufficiently clarified or until the group deliberately and for good reasons decides to address another one. The reason for turning to another question can be because this other question must be answered before progress with the original question is possible. Alternatively, when the group feels that no progress is being made, it can be purposeful to approach the original question from another angle.

During the first years of my Socratic work I tried, whenever we faced the alternative between working with this or that subsidiary question, to fully discuss these alternatives in a Socratic manner. The time and effort this required was always spent in vain. Sometimes the connections revealed in the dialogue make it clear which subsidiary question should be examined next. But there are occasions when several questions emerge from the dialogue, each of which could be followed next. In such situations I have never managed, throughout my Socratic experience, to reach a decision on the basis of convincing reasons. It is as if one wants to arrive at a specific point in otherwise unknown territory, as if one stands in front of an obstacle one could avoid by stepping to the left or right, but ultimately one has no firm basis for one's decision. I have given up any attempt to discuss such decisions to the bitter end when standing at the crossroads. Instead, when such a decision has to be taken in a Socratic Dialogue, I now suggest to the group that it is made according to our preferences, even taking a vote.

Measure five: striving for consensus

It is natural not to be content with the stage reached in the dialogue as long as differences remain about a particular question or not all participants have yet agreed a given statement. In a Socratic Dialogue we want to get beyond mere subjective opinion. That is why we seek out what reasons we have for our statements and then establish whether these reasons are acknowledged by all participants as being sufficient.

Central to Socratic Dialogue is the search for meaning beyond the purely subjective, to strive for valid inter-subjective statements, for truth, as we used to say. When we speak about truth nowadays we are no longer so confident. Striving after truth and claims to have recognised truth in respect of a particular question are often considered presumptuous. On this matter I would like to say the following, looking at it from a Socratic point of view:

Whenever we reach consensus about a statement in a Socratic Dialogue it has a provisional character. For the moment there are no further doubts about the outcome of our effort. Yet a point of view not previously noted can come into our awareness and arouse new doubts. In such a case the proposition has to be tested anew. No statement that emerges can ever avoid the need for further revision.

This recognition rests on an inductive conclusion reached on the basis of experience in reasoning about our statements, in particular in the Socratic Dialogue. The process of winning insights through reflection on experience is determined by the structure of our reasoning capacity, which is the pre-condition for an inductive conclusion.

Could we comprehend the freeing of oneself step-by-step from erroneous ideas and the step-by-step conquering of doubts as advancing towards the truth, fully aware of course that this is always subject to the proviso that pure truth, free from error and the need for revision, is unattainable? Opponents of this view argue that the concept of truth is of no use unless it is free from error. If truth free-from-error does not exist then the manner of speaking 'to get closer to truth devoid of error' is an empty phrase.

Socratic Dialogue does not in fact presuppose the concept of truth 'free from error'. It does presuppose that we can recognise a statement as being false or insufficiently grounded in reason. In that situation we either abandon our statement or seek to modify it until we see no further objections against the modified statement.

In that way we arrive at statements of the quality that we can recognise 'as proven for the time being'. That much we can achieve. We are unable to identify statements of which we can confidently claim that they are error-free or without need of revision. In Socratic Dialogue we strive for the possible and the sought after consensus always has the character of the provisional.

This seems to me a view that in meaning unites the position of Albert Schweitzer on the one hand and Max Born on the other. Schweitzer stated 'I cannot imagine losing the treasured childish belief in truth' whereas Max Born stated

> I believe that ideas, such as absolute correctness, absolute precision, finally valid truth etc are illusions that should never find a place in science... This attractive feature in our thinking seems to me the greatest blessing bestowed on us by modern science. The belief to be possessor of the one and only truth is the deepest root of all evil in the world.

Using the concept of truth critically, even avoiding the word 'truth', does not mean surrendering the idea of truth, which has lent wings to western thought, to science and to critical thought. Quite the contrary, this very idea encourages those motivated by it to engage in critical understanding of themselves. In Socratic Dialogue we are motivated by this idea. It prompts us to describe the experience we have in the Socratic Dialogue with concepts that stand up to critical testing.

I now return to the pedagogical measures with which the Socratic facilitator works and deal with the last one:

Measure six: facilitator interventions
Measure six deals with those interventions by means of which the facilitator steers the dialogue in fruitful directions. By using these measures as well as focusing the dialogue on the current question (measure four above) the facilitator protects the dialogue from the fate of many unguided discussions, including the loss of a clear train of thought, and of the dialogue running into the sand. It is thus important that the facilitator is not burdened by having to defend his own view on the matter being discussed. He is free for his other task: to observe the direction the dialogue takes and to

watch that significant questions are tackled and fruitful contributions are taken up.

Discussion of the six measures

The facilitator interventions discussed above address only *part* of the aim. It remains subordinate to the *main* aim in a Socratic Dialogue, which is to assist participants in their efforts to reach insights. This aim sets boundaries to all facilitator measures, well formulated in measure one above. The facilitator should never disturb the unfolding of the participants' capacity to judge by steering the discussion to move his own judgement on the current question into the foreground.

The use of the blackboard (or flipchart) is not a new pedagogical measure and is an aid for nearly all six measures. In a Socratic Dialogue one attempts to formulate thoughts precisely and then works on these formulations. One often needs to have them in constant view, for which the flipchart record is invaluable. Nelson noted that 'merely by writing up two propositions, two conflicting doctrines' one could 'draw attention to the underlying' wrong presuppositions, 'uncover their misuse and in that process cause the collapse of both propositions'. Nelson showed here that he used the recording of statements as a pedagogical measure to steer the discussion. He also tells us that he steered the attention of the participants towards a particular point the significance of which he had recognised for the investigation, whereas the participants had not yet done so. The act of steering should never encroach on the participants' *own emerging judgement*.

The six pedagogical measures place very different demands on the facilitator. The first two are relatively easy – holding back one's own opinion on the question and guiding the discussion to be anchored in the concrete. Success in withholding his own view requires that the facilitator make an explicit decision in light of understanding the reason for this measure. And in order to ensure that participants clearly illustrate their thoughts by using a personally experienced example, he need only persevere in asking them.

The third measure – working towards shared understanding among all the participants – requires more from the facilitator. It can involve tedious checking with questions like 'could Hans repeat once more how he understood Grete', and then asking Grete 'did he understand you correctly?' The facilitator should not shy away from this if he has the impression that full understanding has not yet been fully achieved. A participant's verbal consent to what another person said is not sufficient guarantee that understanding is reciprocal. 'Yes' can be uttered with more or less conviction. A facilitator who by nature is insensitive to such differences will acquire the knack in the Socratic Dialogue. He will need to pay heed not merely to what the participants say, but also to how they say it and to their overall behaviour during the dialogue. The same applies to the fifth measure: the facilitator must recognise whether some participants agree half-heartedly without really being convinced.

Ensuring that the group focuses on the current question is the fourth measure. To fulfil this task the facilitator has to check for himself whether he still knows which question is being discussed or whether he has lost his overview. If the latter is the case, he has to turn to the group to ask the question: 'I no longer see which question we are talking about. Could someone please tell us?'

To me the sixth measure makes the greatest demands on the facilitator — to recognise and to use fruitful starting points and questions. For this it is important that the facilitator is ahead of the participants in philosophical insights and in experience of the struggle for such insights. Both these attributes are gained only through combining the study of philosophy with long experience in facilitating Socratic Dialogues.

A new facilitator of Socratic Dialogues is well advised to start with topics which are not too far removed from concrete experience. For example, rather than pursuing a question about the abstract principle for solving conflicts justly, it is better to investigate how concrete conflicts can be solved in a fair and just way. Furthermore, a new facilitator does well to concentrate on the first five pedagogical measures and initially to leave aside the sixth. Should the dialogue then develop to a stage when facilitator and participants have lost the overview of connections and no longer recognise fruitful starting points, the dialogue should be terminated. There is little prospect that a rewarding dialogue will still develop in such circumstances.

Referring to the difficulties encountered in Socratic Dialogues, Nelson reminds us how frankly Plato applied his view: 'Yes, Plato breaks off dialogues because the participants have lost their patience.'

The six pedagogical measures make demands on the facilitator. But are they not equally valid for all participants? Through long schooling in Socratic Dialogues it can indeed be achieved that all in the dialogue group pay attention to the six measures. I have reported on one such dialogue, in which I, as facilitator, did not even need to attend to the six demands. The participants themselves kept to them and I could help with writing up sentences on the blackboard. I was also free to introduce my own experiences into the dialogue.

However, Socratic work cannot commence at this level. For a long time the facilitator has a special task. In order that the participants can give their full attention to the point-by-point examination of the *topic* – which alone gives content to the dialogue – the facilitator frees them from concern about the progress of the dialogue. He watches to see that the group fully exploits all points introduced into the dialogue by participants, and that the individual participants make the effort through which insight is gained.

The participants can only gradually reach the stage when they themselves can observe the six pedagogical measures.

Socratic facilitation

I described earlier the measures of intervention with which the facilitator guides the dialogue into fruitful directions or protects it against running into the sand without prospect of any result. These interventions guide the dialogue in directions relevant to the subject under discussion. Every action of the facilitator which seeks to make the participants pay attention to part of a question or a detail, or to consider or leave aside part of a question, is facilitator intervention. In this section I shall use the term 'intervention' in the narrow sense of this definition – not in the broader sense in which the other five pedagogical measures might also be described as facilitator actions of intervention.

Let me give a few examples from my experience of intervention in this narrower sense:

In a seminar on 'the human will', the group failed to make real headway on the question of why Karl's will to help Dieter did not prevail against Karl's own opposing inner resistance. On that occasion I suggested that we should first look at the case of a will that prevails against inner resistance and then, with the insights gained, return to consider Karl's will which had not prevailed. The result of this was that the significance of value insights for the strength of will emerged impressively and that the group gained this important insight. It is doubtful whether the group would have gained this insight had we examined only Karl's unsuccessful will.

In another dialogue Käthe spoke of 'self-confirmation', and as examples gave various experiences such as enjoyment of nature and satisfaction over one's own successful achievement. Evidently she had in mind an idea of a basic human experience that manifested itself in various ways, but which she did not at first clearly identify. When a multitude of further examples of this basic experience had been put forward, I insisted that the group seek out those characteristics that were common to all these examples. This led to recognition of the nature of that basic experience and to finding an appropriate description of it.

In another seminar on truth in mathematics, the group's activity flagged: their interest in the truth problem of mathematics was not very strong and the difficulties of the problem were considerable. Had I at the time seen a course of action by which I might have steered the dialogue in a fruitful direction I would have done so to spare the group pointless effort. However, as I reported under the keyword of 'Failed Intervention', I did not then see such a possibility. Measures of intervention are therefore helpful steps by which the facilitator can steer the dialogue onto a fruitful path or away from a hopeless one.

Their characteristic is: Take this step first, and then you will make progress. They in no way relieve the group from taking the step on their own. Neither do they indicate to the group what result the step will lead to in the facilitator's opinion.

A good master will spare his disciple the repeated experience of being unable to do something because he has faced him with excessively difficult tasks. That would destroy his self-confidence and enjoyment of the work. Instead the teacher will face his disciple with tasks that fully challenge, but do not exceed the disciple's strength and, in the course of his educational development will progressively increase the difficulty of those tasks.

This general principle, valid for all teaching and education, also underpins Socratic teaching. The Socratic teacher will stretch the students' capacities, exposing them to intellectual effort and even to surviving barren stretches – as testified by my seminar reports. He will try to spare the students failure in the face of excessive difficulties and the mere experience of incapability. I have once experienced prolonged Socratic work that ended in a total absence of outcomes and in depression for all involved – facilitator and participants. That was not a good experience for any of us, though it was intended to induce pleasure in thinking for oneself or enhance confidence in the power of one's own thought. The Socratic teacher will be out to ensure that his students themselves have the experience that through strenuous joint efforts one can achieve essential insights; he will endeavour to transmit this experience with as much depth and breadth as the circumstances permit. Measures of intervention by the teacher should serve this one and only goal and should be evaluated exclusively according to whether or not they actually serve this goal.

As for letting participants win insights of as much depth and breadth as possible under the given circumstances, I can basically see two constraints that limit what is possible. The first concerns the intellectual levels and interests of the participants, and the second is the time available for the work.

The importance of the first of these two factors emerged clearly, for example, from the situation in the seminar about truth in mathematics, when it became apparent that the interest of the participants in the problem was too weak for them to make the effort required for surmounting the difficulties. At the time the group had to decide whether to give up the subject 'truth in mathematics' and instead tackle the topic 'truth between people'. In my report on that situation and on the reaching of the decision, I said: 'I was determined not to intervene and hold the group back in any way should it decide to discontinue the examination of mathematical truth. Without the motivation to carry out that investigation, the group could not surmount the difficulties, and I could not implant that motivation in them from outside.' Faced with a choice between several suggestions, the group eventually decided in favour of continuing the examination of mathematical truth, and it was obvious that they were now motivated. The work was then advanced to a point where all probably felt what I expressed: 'After all, the drudgery was worthwhile.'

The significance of the second factor, the time available, may also be illustrated by an example: When Paul drew attention to physiological criteria during a discussion about the phenomenon of heightened intensity of inner life, I intervened and put this idea aside with the argument that we were at that moment investigating a phenomenon of inner experience and that the examination of outer processes, such as physiological ones, could not help us in this. My motivation for this *intervention*, of putting aside Paul's idea was as follows: He was raising a new significant set of problems concerning the differentiation and the interacting relations between external and internal processes, of external and internal experience, problems that could not be treated briefly. The time available to the seminar would probably have been insufficient to clarify this new problem as well as the basic experience we were concerned with, the experience that Käthe had in mind and – not quite accurately – called 'self-confirmation'. I decided that we should remain with the examination of that basic experience rather than address the problem of external and internal processes.

It was appropriate that we had at that point to consider the time available to us and decide which of the two problems we preferred to discuss. But the manner in which I intervened was not correct. I should have set out to the group the situation as I saw it – that we were facing two important problems that could not be tackled in a hurry and that probably we would not have enough time to clarify both. Then the group should have decided which of the two problems it wished to address first, aware of the risk that we might not manage to discuss the other.

Facilitator intervention invariably aims at a decision on the path to be followed, when the facilitator regards a particular path as suitable. Good interventions, from a pedagogical perspective, are those where the group is aware of the facilitator's reasons for his suggestion, and makes the decision by itself. It involves the facilitator in steering the group specifically to bring about the decision of the group. Bad from a pedagogical point of view are interventions which the group does not notice ('blind interventions') or when it senses that the facilitator wants something from the group but does not know what. Good interventions were my proposal to investigate the topic of will when it successfully asserted itself against inner resistance, as well as my bringing about the group's decision on whether it wished to discontinue the examination of mathematical truth. I made a bad intervention at the beginning of the seminar about will, when I gave emphasis to the formulation of two statements on the blackboard by underlining them. I was aiming at pointing participants to the general problem recognisable behind the specific formulations.

I can see yet another criterion for the pedagogical assessment of measures of intervention. In terms of the pedagogy any intervention is questionable that anticipates an insight which the group could have arrived at by itself. This was the case in the example about 'self-confirmation' cited above. The group had brought together a multitude of diverse inner experiences as examples of what Käthe had called 'self-confirmation'. By calling on the group to search for the common characteristic to these inner experiences, I anticipated the group's own realisation that these experiences had to have a common characteristic. I would have done better not to do so but merely to keep the group focused on the collected experiences. Somehow it would have occurred to them to characterise that which was common to those experiences by identifying a specific aspect.

However, these two criteria for distinguishing pedagogically good from pedagogically questionable interventions do not suffice to resolve the fundamental pedagogical problem of facilitator intervention: Is not a Socratic Dialogue which entirely abandons interventions in the above-defined narrow sense fundamentally preferable, from a pedagogical point of view, to one that makes use of them? In discussions on the Socratic Method I have often encountered an unclearly reasoned opposition to measures of intervention, an opposition that might be expressed by the above question. Or, to put it more precisely: Does not Socratic teaching that dispenses with measures of intervention train a person's own thinking and lead to insights more effectively than Socratic teaching operating with facilitator intervention? That would be Socratic teaching in which the teacher does not reveal his own view on the problem under discussion, but works solely to uphold the following pedagogical requirements for participants: keeping the dialogue anchored in concrete experience; ensuring that participants really understand one another; focusing on a subsidiary question until it is solved; striving towards consensus. During such a dialogue or seminar the facilitator would allow a fruitful forward-leading point in the dialogue to be left aside, unused, should the participants not have noticed its value.

The dialogue reports presented in this book do not show such reticence by the facilitator; they only describe Socratic Dialogues working with the use of interventions. I personally have never experimented with abandoning the intervention role because the problem formulated above did not become clear to me until later. The fundamental pedagogical problem of facilitation can surely be resolved by experience alone; only by comparing experiences of the Socratic Method renouncing facilitator intervention with others which use measures of intervention as described in my reports. A comparative experiment of Socratic teaching using and not using intervention has not, to my knowledge, so far been made.

On the strength of experience, however, I believe I can venture the following statement: The pedagogical goal of allowing the dialogue participants to gain insights which have as much depth and breadth as possible – taking into account the intellectual levels and interests of the participants and of the time available to the group – this goal cannot be attained without facilitator intervention. The examples of intervention in this chapter demonstrate this fact. Every one of these facilitator actions helped us advance some way towards that goal.

However, this does not answer the fundamental pedagogical question: could not a form of Socratic Method that dispenses with intervention in the narrow sense defined above, and hence also with participants winning some good insightful individual experiences, achieve more in terms of strengthening the type of thinking that leads to insights? More than the Socratic Method that makes use of intervention, as described in my reports?

As Socratic Dialogue participants become more experienced, the problem of intervention eventually disappears. The Socratic activity loses the character of a learning exercise in which the facilitator is the teacher and becomes a conversation among equals. [Heckmann described one such dialogue in another chapter of his book. eds]. In that dialogue, there were no facilitator interventions, nor did the facilitator use any other pedagogical measures. The facilitator was an equal dialogue participant, merely performing the ancillary service of writing on the blackboard.

13

THE SOCRATIC METHOD
AN INTRODUCTION TO THE ESSAY OF NELSON

Fernando Leal

Twenty-five hundred years ago a humble stonemason living in a small town of a few thousand souls, invented a wholly new way for people to engage in conversation. His name was Socrates and his invention has been known ever since as the Socratic Dialogue. Socrates had apparently no particular name for it; and the expression 'Socratic Dialogue', as far as we can say, was actually introduced into common usage not to describe what Socrates did in the streets of Athens but as a conventional label for a new kind of drama or play featuring a funny character. The character, called Socrates, typically engaged in what is by all accounts a peculiar kind of conversation with other characters. The emergence of Socratic Dialogues in that sense is one of the reasons why most people tend to think of a Socratic Dialogue as fiction not reality. However, the main message of Nelson's essay is that Socratic Dialogues can be more than just a literary fiction. People can still engage in conversations of the kind that Socrates invented twenty-five hundred years ago in Athens. Socratic Dialogue can be as great as it was when it was first devised and practised by Socrates and his fellow-citizens long before it was fictionalised, ie converted into something you enjoy reading but would never dream of actually doing.

Conversation, talking to each other, chatting away, – is probably the activity which occupies most waking hours of most human beings. It is both a necessity and generally an agreeable thing to do. A whole branch of social science does its research on the assumption that social life is not only absolutely dependent on conversations but constructed out of them. Conversations come in many kinds. Some of them may be natural in that recognisable specimens can be found in all cultures, while other kinds seem to be peculiar to only some ways of life, some societies, some traditions. Thus to have something like a discussion over a beer, a teatime chat, a pub argument, or a polite conversation, you need to be a member of a certain tribe, so to speak. Yet traditional ways of talking share a feature with natural ways, if indeed there are natural ways, namely, that nobody in particular can be made responsible for them, no nameable individual can be said to have devised them. One of the very few methods of conversation which are thus traceable to a particular person is the Socratic Dialogue. There is certainly nothing like it in nature; and, although a cultural product, it is not anonymous like most cultural products. It bears the personal stamp of that stonemason who was born in Athens, lived in Athens and died in Athens.

Also, like most cultural products, the Socratic Dialogue has evolved. It may well have started to evolve already in the hands of its inventor as he practised it over the years. This may partly explain why Greek dramatic pieces called Socratic Dialogues produced such different portrayals of the method as found in Plato, Xenophon, Aristophanes and others. Intrigued by these differences, scholars have been trying to find out who the real Socrates was; and a mighty dispute among the pundits has emerged which may never finish. However, at least from a practical point of view, it is vastly more interesting to recover the Socratic Dialogue itself, which we cannot do if we don't dare to engage in conversation along roughly Socratic lines. Some archaeologists have discovered the techniques for building Stone Age artefacts by actually building them. This involves some trial and error for sure; but there is no substitute for it. Similarly, our best chance to see what Socrates was about is to talk to each other in the way he devised. We may have to use trial and error. The conversations we engage in by trying to follow his example may change as a consequence; so be it, the fruits we collect are too precious, the promise of more and better too alluring, the philosophical lessons we learn too powerful and profound. And it is anyway in the nature of all human inventions not to stay put, but to invite constant reform and elaboration.

Quite independently of the fact that practising the Socratic Dialogue may help to recover what was unquestionably a great cultural invention, it has enormous value in itself, as anybody can witness who has tried. It is useless to try to describe what it is or what it does to you. It has to be experienced. But it's not easy and not always comfortable. It calls for tenacity, discipline, patience, humour and intelligence. It is hard work. The main thing is to listen, to listen to other people and to listen to yourself. And when you listen to others, it is not only to know whether they have understood you, but to know whether you have understood them. Only then will you enable them to listen to themselves; and if everything goes the way it should, then what you have done unto them they will do unto you: they will be listening to you in order to know whether they have understood you, and so they will enable you to listen to yourself. Not your ego, not your reputation, not your erudition. Just yourself. The Socratic work is a work of cooperation, a way of thinking together, of growing together.

Just yourself, I say. For the main assumption behind a Socratic Dialogue, the philosophical bottom line, is that deep inside ourselves we have knowledge about the most important things which should concern human beings, namely how we ought to live. This is a peculiar kind of knowledge, calling for a peculiar kind of conversation. But knowledge it is, not just belief or conviction or persuasion or ideology. All these things do exist; but all are barriers to knowledge. They project shadows on our most vital concerns; they obscure the issues; they obstruct the view. In sum, they don't let us think for ourselves. All sorts of voices talk within us, the thousand voices of indoctrination and convention and dogma, the thousand voices of prestige and complacency and fear of other people's opinion of us. Which is why, in a Socratic Dialogue, nobody can be given a voice if not present in the dialogue, nothing can be discussed if there is not at least one person who actually stands behind it. Some people may find this unreasonable. My answer to them is: don't judge before trying it. That way lies dogmatism.

There is a basic assumption behind the practice of Socratic Dialogue. Namely, that it is worth our while to talk about the most important things, about how we ought to live. This assumption is totally against the spirit of the times. Most people take a relativistic view with respect to the most important things. They tend to believe that nobody can know the truth about these things, and even that there is no truth to be known about them. I understand that and to some degree share the attitude. We need tolerance; there has been far too much dogmatism and imposition in the history of humankind. Conquest, burning, judgement, condemnation and censorship have always been with us, oppressing and destroying whole peoples and cultures. In so far as relativism is a protest against such horrors, it can do good. Philosophers have argued that it is theoretically bankrupt because it is inconsistent. The argument is surely correct, but also, to me at least, uninteresting. What concerns me is that the practical usefulness of relativism is quite limited, for it only helps us as long as we are not involved in a practical situation in which there is disagreement on what is good or what one ought to do.

In practical situations you are just not considering the options, viewing things from the outside, from the third-person perspective (the actors being, for you, a he, she or them). You are not just an observer but an actor: you have to do something, you are interested in the outcome, and often in one outcome in particular. You have a first-person perspective (the actor being, for you, not a he or she but an I). Relativism is of no help at all here. What dialogue does for you is to convert the solitary first-person perspective into a second-person one, thus increasing the power of thinking. Here the actor in the practical situation becomes a thou or a you, with whom you can talk. But in order to do that, you have to assume that it is worth your while to talk, to engage in conversation as does everybody involved. And this is where, from being a force for good (in the shape of tolerance) tolerance comes to be an obstacle to dialogue. If everything is relative and everyone is entitled to their own opinion, because after all there are only opinions, then why should we bother to talk or to listen?

Although Socratic Dialogues have traditionally been considered fictions, there may always have been people who tried to practise them in some way. But the German philosopher Leonard Nelson was evidently the first to do it in a public and systematic way. He thought of Socratic Dialogue as a unique way to learn to philosophise, an antidote to and even a political weapon against dogmatism, and a royal path to ethical truth; and he institutionalised it in such a way that his students and political associates could work on it, allowing for interesting modifications and additions.

As Nelson describes it in the essay that follows – originally a lecture given in 1922 to the Pedagogical Society in Göttingen – the Socratic Dialogue was first used as a pedagogic technique in university seminars in inter-war Germany. Afterwards Nelson came to use it outside of college, both with adults in political organisations and with children in school. When Nelson died shortly before the Nazis came to power, his followers continued to practise the Socratic Dialogue both in Germany and in the countries where they became political refugees. In the post-war period, the Socratic work has steadily grown and nowadays it is a dearly appreciated activity in which hundreds of people have engaged and keep engaging, year after year, in Germany, in the Netherlands, and more recently in Britain. It is most emphatically not a fiction. What Socrates initiated in Athens twenty-five hundred years ago is still going strong at the beginning of the new millennium. The torch has been passed on.

THE SOCRATIC METHOD

Leonard Nelson

As a faithful disciple of Socrates and of his great successor Plato, I find it rather difficult to justify my acceptance of your invitation to talk to you about the Socratic Method. You know the Socratic Method as a method of teaching philosophy. But philosophy is different from other subjects of instruction; in Plato's own words:

> It does not at all admit of verbal expression like other studies, but as a result of continued application to the subject itself and communion therewith, it is brought to birth in the soul, as suddenly as light that is kindled by a leaping spark, and thereafter it nourishes itself.[1]

I therefore find myself in a quandary, not unlike that of a violinist who, when asked how he goes about playing the violin, can of course demonstrate his art but cannot explain his technique in abstract terms.

The Socratic Method, then, is the art of teaching not philosophy but philosophising, the art not of teaching about philosophers but of making philosophers of the students. So, in order to give a true idea of the Socratic Method, I should halt my discourse right here and, instead of lecturing to you, take up with you a philosophical problem and deal with it according to the Socratic Method. But what did Plato say? Only 'continued application to the subject itself and communion therewith' kindle the light of philosophical cognition.

Despite the short time at my disposal I shall nevertheless venture a description of the Socratic Method and attempt through words to bring home to you its meaning and significance. I justify this compromise by limiting my task, the sole object of my exposition being to direct your attention to this method of teaching and thereby to promote an appreciation of it.

A person who knows no more about the Grand Inquisitor's speech in Dostoevsky's novel, *The Brothers Karamazov*, than that it is a magnificent discussion of a fundamental ethical problem, knows little enough about it; yet that little will make him more disposed to read the speech attentively. Similarly, whoever looks at the memorial tablet here in the former Physics Institute [Göttingen] that tells of the first electric telegraph invented by Gauss and Wilhelm Weber and how it served to connect that institute with the astronomical observatory will at least feel inclined to follow up the history of this invention with greater reverence. And so I hope that in presenting my subject I, too, may arouse your interest in the significant and, for all its simplicity, profound method that bears the name of the Athenian sage to whom we owe its invention.

A stepchild of philosophy, slighted and rejected, the Socratic Method has survived only in name beside its more popular older sister, the more insinuating and more easily manipulated dogmatic method.

You may perhaps suspect me of a personal inclination for the younger of the two sisters. And, indeed, I freely confess that the longer I enjoy her company, the more I am captivated by her charms; so that it has become a matter of chivalry with me to lead back to life she who has been forgotten and pronounced dead, and to win her here that place of honour hitherto reserved for the wanton sister who, though dead at heart, has time and again appeared all decked out.

Let me add, however – and this much I hope to demonstrate to you today – that it is not blind partiality that actuates me; it is the inner worth of her whose appearance is so plain that attracts me to her. But, you say, her sad fate – being disdained by the overwhelming majority of philosophers – could not have been undeserved and it is therefore idle to try to breathe new life into her by artificial means.

In reply I shall not resort to the general proposition that history shows no pre-established harmony between merit and success, for, indeed, the success or failure of a *method* as a means to an end is a very real test of its value.

However, a fair judgement requires consideration of a preliminary question, namely, whether a particular science is so far advanced that the solution of its problems is sought in a prescribed way; in other words, whether generally valid methods are recognised in it.

In mathematics and in the natural sciences based on it this question of method was long ago decided affirmatively. There is not a mathematician who is not familiar with and who does not employ the progressive method. All serious research in the natural sciences makes use of the inductive method. In fact, method enjoys in these sciences a recognition so unchallenged and matter of course that the students following its guidance are often hardly conscious of the assured course of their researches. All dispute about methods here turns exclusively on their reliability and fruitfulness. If, in this field, a method is dropped or retains merely a historic interest, the presumption is justified that it can offer nothing more to research.

It is quite otherwise, however, in a science where everyone still claims the right to make his [sic] own laws and rules, where methodological directives are evaluated *ab initio* as temporally or individually conditioned, subject only to historical appraisal. With luck one method may find favour and for a time determine the direction of future work. But in such a science errors, concomitants of every scientific achievement, do not inspire efforts in the already established direction to correct the defects; errors here are looked upon as faults of construction and must give way to entirely new structures, which in their turn all too soon meet the same fate.

What passes for philosophical science is still in this youthful stage of development. In this judgement I have the support of Windelband, the renowned historian of philosophy. He tells us that 'even among the philosophers who claim a special method for their science' – and by no means all philosophers make such a claim – 'there is not the least agreement concerning this 'philosophical method'.'[2]

This conclusion appears the more depressing in view of his previous admission that it is impossible to establish a constant criterion even for the very subject matter of philosophy.

In view of this, one wonders what such philosophers really think of their science. At any rate, in this anarchy the question is left open whether the disesteem into which a philosophical theory falls in itself proves that the theory is scientifically worthless. For how can we expect to judge the scientific value or lack of value of a philosophical achievement when generally valid criteria for judging it do not exist?

Now, it is not that the diversity of the *results* made it difficult for philosophers to set up a systematic guide to their science. On the contrary, the great philosophical truths have been from the beginning the common property of all the great thinkers. Here, then, a common starting point was provided. But the verification of these results according to unequivocal rules that preclude arbitrariness and even the mere formulation of the pertinent methodological task with definiteness and precision are both tasks in the general interest of philosophy which have thus far been given so little attention that we must not be surprised that the devoted efforts of a few men to satisfy this interest have proved in vain. True, the lifelong work of Socrates and of Kant in the service of this methodological task has earned immeasurable historical glory. But, as far as its revolutionary significance for the establishment of philosophy as a science is concerned, it has remained sterile and ineffectual.

Twice in its history there was some prospect of getting philosophy out of its groping stage and onto the certain path of science. The ancient world punished the first courageous attempt with death: Socrates was condemned as a corrupter of youth. The modern world disdains to execute the heretic. It has passed sentence by 'going beyond' Kant – to let Windelband speak once more.[3]

But there is no need for laboured interpretation to appreciate the significance of these two men. They themselves stressed the meaning of their endeavours, explicitly and unceasingly. As everyone knows, Socrates constructed no system. Time and again he admitted his not-knowing. He met every assertion with an invitation to seek the ground of its truth. As the *Apology* shows, he 'questioned and examined and cross-examined'[4] his fellow citizens, not to convey a new truth to them in the manner of an instructor but only to point out the path along which it might be found.

His ethical doctrine, in so far as this designation is appropriate to his inquiries, is based on the proposition that virtue can be taught, or, to put it in more precise terms, that ethics is a science. Socrates did not develop this science, because the initial question, '*How* do I gain knowledge about virtue?' continued to absorb him. He held fast to this initial question. He accepted the absence of fruitful results with composure, without a trace of scepticism as to the soundness of his method, unshakable in the conviction that with his question he was, in spite of everything, on the only right road.

All subsequent philosophy, with the sole exception of Plato, stands helpless before that memorable fact. Plato took over and adhered to the method of Socrates, even after his own researches had carried him far beyond the results reached by his master. He adopted it with all its imperfections. He failed to eliminate its weaknesses and inflexibilities, surely not because of reverence for the memory of his teacher but because he could not overcome these defects. Like Socrates, he was guided by a feeling for truth. Having dealt so boldly with the content of the Socratic philosophy that philosophical philologists are still quarrelling about what is Socratic in Plato's doctrine and what Platonic, he turned this boldness into homage by putting all his own discoveries into the mouth of his great teacher. But he paid Socrates even greater homage by clothing these discoveries in the uneven, often dragging, often digressive form of the Socratic Dialogue, burdening his own teachings with his teacher's faults. In this manner, of course, he safeguarded the yet unmined treasure and thus gave posterity the opportunity of taking possession of it anew and of developing its riches.

But in vain. Today, after two thousand years, opinion on Socrates is more uncertain and more divided than ever. Over the judgement of an expert like Joel, that Socrates was 'the first and perhaps the last quite genuine, *quite pure* philosopher',[5] there is Heinrich Maier's statement 'that Socrates has been labelled as what he quite certainly was not, a philosopher'.[6]

This difference of opinion has its roots in the inadequacy of the criticism, which still exercises its ingenuity on the conclusions of Socrates' philosophy. But as these conclusions were handed down only indirectly and perhaps were never even given definite form by Socrates, so remain exposed to the most contradictory interpretations. Where criticism touches on the method, it either praises trivialities or assigns the value of the Socratic Method exclusively to the personality of Socrates, as shown in the opinion voiced by Wilamowitz in his *Platon*: 'The Socratic Method without Socrates is no more than a pedagogy that, aping how some inspired spiritual leader clears his throat and spits, bottles his alleged method and then imagines it is dispensing the water of life.'[7]

If Socrates' philosophy, lively and rooted in concrete problems as it was, found no emulators, it is little wonder then that the truth content of Kant's far more abstract methodological investigations failed to be understood and adopted – except by those few who comprehended his doctrine and developed it further, but who in their turn were pushed completely into the background by the irresistible *Zeitgeist* and passed over by history. The preconditions were lacking for the realisation that Kant's critical method was the resumption of Socratic-Platonic philosophising, and for the acceptance of the *Critique of Pure Reason* as a 'treatise on the method', which its author, according to his own words, intended it to be.[8]

In addition to this treatise on method, Kant produced a system. He enriched the broad domain of philosophy with an abundance of fruitful results. It was these results that became the subject of controversy; but the hope of a satisfactory settlement was bound to remain illusory as long as no attempt was made to retrace the creative path by which Kant had reached his conclusions. Dogmatism remained dominant, more triumphant than ever in the erection of arbitrary systems that vied with one another in bizarreness and estranged public interest altogether from the sober and critical philosophising of the Kantian period. Such fragments of Kant's results as were transplanted to this alien soil could not thrive there and maintained only an artificial existence, thanks to a fancy for the history of philosophy that displaced philosophy itself.

Why is it, asked Kant, that nothing is being done to prevent the 'scandal' which, 'sooner or later, is sure to become obvious even to the masses, as the result of the disputes in which metaphysicians ... without critique inevitably become involved.'[9]

It is manifestly the aim of every science to verify its judgements by reducing them to more general propositions, which themselves must be made certain. We can then proceed from these principles to the erection of the scientific system through logical inference. However difficult this may be in its details, in its essence it is accomplished in all sciences by the same method, that of progressive reasoning. The methodological problems are encountered in every science where the regress from the particular to the general has to be accomplished, where the task is to secure the most fundamental propositions, the most general principles.

The brilliant development of the science of mathematics and its universally acknowledged advance are explained by the fact that its principles – ignoring for the moment the problems of axiomatics – are easily grasped by the consciousness. They are intuitively clear and thus completely evident, so evident that, as Hilbert recently remarked on this same platform, mathematical comprehension can be forced on everyone. The mathematician does not even have to perform the laborious regress to these principles. He is free to start from arbitrarily formed concepts and go on confidently to propositions; in short, he can immediately proceed systematically, and in this sense dogmatically. He can do so because the fact that his concepts lend themselves to construction is a criterion of their reality, a sure indication that his theory does not deal with mere fictions.

The natural sciences, however, do not enjoy this advantage. The laws underlying natural phenomena can be uncovered only by induction. But since induction proceeds from the observation of facts, from which accidental elements are eliminated by experimentation; since, moreover, all events in space and in time are susceptible of mathematical calculation; and, finally, since the theoretical generalisations obtained are, as empirical propositions, subject to check by confirmatory or contradictory experience, the natural sciences have, in close relation to mathematics, likewise achieved the ascent to the scientific level. Where this claim is still contested, as in biology, the metaphysical premises within the inductive science are involved. There, to be sure, we find at once the confusion that is encountered whenever we pass into the realm of philosophy.

Philosophy does not rest on principles that are self-evident truths. On the contrary, its principles are the focus of obscurity, uncertainty, and controversy. There is unanimity only with respect to the concrete application of these principles. But the moment we try to disregard the particular instance of application and to isolate the principles from experience, that is, if we try to formulate them in pure abstraction, our search gets lost in metaphysical darkness unless we illuminate our way by the artificial light of a method.

Under these circumstances one would expect to find interest in the problem of method nowhere so great as among philosophers. It should be noted, however, that the consideration just put forward itself depends on a methodological point of view. It raises, in advance of any philosophical speculation proper, the question of the nature of philosophical cognition; and it is only through this preliminary question that light is shed on the real content of the problems besetting philosophy.

★ ★ ★

Let us pause here a moment and take a closer look at the concept of the method with which we are concerned. What, precisely, is meant by a method that subjects the thinking of philosophers to its rules? Obviously, it is something other than just the rules of logical thinking. Obedience to the laws of logic is an indispensable precondition of any science. The essential factor distinguishing a method of philosophy can therefore not be found in the fact that it avails itself of logic. That would too narrowly circumscribe the function devolving on it. On the other hand, the demands made on method must not go too far, nor should the impossible be expected of it, namely, the creative increase of philosophical knowledge.

The function to be performed by the philosophical method is nothing other than making secure the contemplated regress to principles, for without the guidance of method, such a regress would be merely a leap in the dark and would leave us where we were before – prey to the arbitrary.

But how to find the clarity requisite for discovering such a guide, since nothing is clear save only judgements relative to individual instances? For these judgements the concrete use of our intelligence, as applied in every empirical judgement in science and in daily life, suffices. Once we go beyond these judgements, how can we orient ourselves at all? The difficulty that seems to be present here is resolved upon critical examination of these empirical judgements. Each of them comprises, in addition to the particular data supplied by observation, a cognition hidden in the very form of the judgement. This cognition, however, is not separately perceived, but by virtue of it we already actually assume and apply the principle we seek.

To give a commonplace illustration: If we were here to discuss the meaning of the philosophical concept of substance, we should most probably become involved in a hopeless dispute, in which the sceptics would very likely soon get the best of it. But if, on the conclusion of our debate, one of the sceptics failed to find his overcoat beside the door where he had hung it, he would hardly reconcile himself to the unfortunate loss of his coat on the ground that it simply confirmed his philosophical doubt of the permanence of substance. Like anyone else hunting for a lost object, the sceptic assumes in the judgement that motivates his search the universal truth that no thing can become nothing, and thus, without being conscious of the inconsistency with his doctrine, he employs the metaphysical principle of the permanence of substance.

Or, suppose we discussed the universal validity of the idea of justice. Our discussion would have the same outcome and once more seem to favour the sceptic who denies the universal validity of ethical truths. When, however, this sceptic reads in his evening paper that farmers are still holding back grain deliveries to exploit a favourable market and that bread will therefore have to be rationed again, he will not readily be disposed to suppress his indignation on the ground that there is no common principle of right applicable to producer and consumer. Like everyone else he condemns profiteering and thereby demonstrates that in fact he acknowledges the metaphysical assumption of equal rights to the satisfaction of interests, regardless of the favourableness or unfavourableness of any individual's personal situation.

It is the same with all experiential judgements. If we inquire into the conditions of their possibility, we come upon more general propositions that constitute the basis of the particular judgements passed. By analysing conceded judgements we go back to their presuppositions. We operate regressively from the consequences to the reason. In this regression we eliminate the accidental facts to which the particular judgement relates and by this separation bring into relief the originally obscure assumption that lies at the bottom of the judgement on the concrete instance. The regressive method of abstraction, which serves to disclose philosophical principles, produces no new knowledge either of facts or of laws. It merely utilises reflection to transform into clear concepts what reposed in our reason as an original possession and made itself obscurely heard in every individual judgement.

It seems as though this discussion has carried us far from our real theme, the method of teaching philosophy. Let us then find the connection. We have discovered philosophy to be the sum total of those universal rational truths that become clear only through reflection. To philosophise, then, is simply to isolate these rational truths with our intellect and to express them in general judgements.

What implications does this hold for the teaching of philosophy? When expressed in words, these universal truths will be heard, but it does not necessarily follow that they will be comprehended. We can understand them only when, beginning with their application in our judgements, we then personally undertake the regress to the premises of these empirical judgements and recognise in them our own presuppositions.

It is accordingly impossible to communicate philosophy, the sum total of these philosophical principles, by instruction as we communicate historical facts or even geometrical theorems. The facts of history as such are not objects of insight; they can only be noted.

True, the principles of mathematics are comprehensible, but we gain insight into them without treading the circuitous path of our own creative thinking. They become immediately evident as soon as attention is directed to their content. The mathematics teacher who anticipates his pupil's independent investigation by presenting these principles in lectures does not thereby impair their clarity. In this case the pupil is able to follow even though he does not himself travel the exploratory path to them. To what extent such instruction makes sure that the pupil follows with real comprehension is of course another question.

But to present philosophy in this manner is to treat it as a science of facts that are to be accepted as such. The result is at best a mere history of philosophy. For what the instructor communicates is not philosophical truth itself but merely the fact that he or somebody else considers this or that to be a philosophical truth. In claiming that he is teaching philosophy, he deceives both himself and his students.

The teacher who seriously wishes to impart philosophical insight can aim only at teaching the art of philosophising. He can do no more than show his students how to undertake, each for himself, the laborious regress that alone affords insight into basic principles. If there is such a thing at all as instruction in philosophy, it can only be instruction in doing one's own thinking; more precisely, in the independent practice of the art of abstraction. The meaning of my initial remark, that the Socratic Method, as a method of instruction in philosophy, is the art not of teaching philosophy but of teaching philosophising, will now become clear. But we have gone further than that. We also know now that, in order to succeed, this art must be guided by the rules of the regressive method.

We have still to examine the subsidiary question, whether this, the only appropriate method of teaching philosophy, is rightfully called the Socratic Method. For my earlier references to the significance of Socrates bore only on the fact that his procedure pertained to method.

To begin with, it goes without saying that this way of teaching is full of faults. Every intelligent college freshman reading Plato's dialogues raises the objection that Socrates, at the most decisive points, engages in monologues and that his pupils are scarcely more than yes men – at times, as Fries remarks, one does not even quite see how they arrived at the 'yes'.[10] In addition to these didactic defects, there are grave philosophical errors, so that we often find ourselves concurring in the dissenting opinions of some of the participants.

In order to reach a conclusion concerning truth and error, the valuable and the valueless, let us take another glance at Plato's account. No one has appraised Socrates' manner of teaching and its effects on his pupils with greater objectivity or deeper knowledge of human nature. Whenever the reader is moved to protest against long-windedness or hair splitting in the conversations, against the monotony of the deductions, against the futility of the battle of words, a like protest arises at once from some participant in the dialogue. How openly Plato allows pupils to voice their displeasure, their doubt, their boredom – just think of the railing of Callicles in the *Gorgias*.[11] He even has conversations breaking off because the patience of the participants is exhausted; and the reader's judgement is by no means always in favour of Socrates. But does this criticism reveal anything except the sovereign assurance with which Plato stands by the method of his teacher for all its shortcomings? Is there any better proof of confidence in the inherent value of a cause than to depict it with all its imperfections, certain that it will nevertheless prevail? Plato's attitude toward his teacher's work is like that displayed toward Socrates, the man, in the well-known oration by Alcibiades in the *Symposium*. There, by contrasting the uncouth physical appearance of Socrates with his inner nature, he makes his noble personality shine forth with greater radiance and compares him to a Silenus who bears within him the mark of the gods.

What, then, is the positive element in the work of Socrates? Where do we find the beginnings of the art of teaching philosophy? Surely not in the mere transition from the rhetoric of the sophists to the dialogue with pupils, even though we ignore the fact that, as I have already indicated, the questions put by Socrates are for the most part leading questions eliciting no more than 'Undoubtedly, Socrates!' 'Truly, so it is, by Zeus! How could it be otherwise?'

But suppose Socrates' philosophical ardour and his awkwardness had allowed the pupils more self-expression. We should still have to inquire first into the deeper significance of the dialogue in philosophical instruction and into the lessons to be derived from Plato's use of it.

We find dialogue employed as an art form in fiction and drama and as a pedagogic form in instruction. Theoretically these forms are separable but actually we require of every conversation liveliness, clarity, and beauty of expression, as well as espousal of truth, decisiveness, and strength of conviction. Even though the emphasis varies, we like to recognise the teacher in the artist and the artist in the teacher.

We must furthermore distinguish between a conversation reduced to writing – even though it is a reproduction of actual speech – and a real conversation carried on between persons. Conversations that are written down lose their original liveliness, 'like the flower in the botanist's case'. If, in spite of this, we are to find them satisfactory, the atmosphere must be spiritualised and purified, standards must be raised; and then there may come forth some rare and admirable production as the conversation of the Grand Inquisitor, which is carried on with a silent opponent who by his silence defeats him.

Conversation as a pedagogic form, however, must sound like actual talk; otherwise it does not fulfil its task of being a model and guide. To catch, in the mirror of a written reproduction, the fleeting form of such talk with its irregularities, to strike the mean between fidelity to the sense and fidelity to the word – this is a problem that can perhaps be solved didactically; but the solution, serving as it does a definite purpose, will rarely meet the demands of free art and therefore as a whole will nearly always produce a mixed impression. I know of only a few didactic conversations in literature from which this discord has been even partially eliminated. I have in mind, for instance, some passages in the three well known dialogues by Solovyeff; then there is the Socratic Dialogue with which the American socialist writer Bellamy opens his didactic novel *Looking Backward*; and finally – by no means the least successful – the conversations in August Niemann's novel *Bakchen und Thyrsosträger*, which is imbued with the true Socratic spirit.

To the difficulty just described one must add another, more basic objection, that to reduce the evolving didactic conversation to writing borders on the absurd. For by offering the solution along with the problem, the transcription violates, with respect to the reader, the rule of individual effort and honesty and thus, as Socrates puts it in the *Phaedrus*, imparts to the novice 'the appearance of wisdom, not true wisdom'.[12] Such writing has meaning only for those to whom it recalls their own intellectual efforts. On all others it acts as an obstacle to insight – it seduces them into the naive notion that, as Socrates says further on, 'anything in writing will be clear and certain'.[13] Thus Plato speaks of his own 'perplexity and uncertainty'[14] in setting down his thoughts in writing.

> It does not at all admit of verbal expression ... But were I to undertake this task it would not, as I think, prove a good thing for men, save for some few who are able to discover the truth themselves with but little instruction; for as to the rest, some it would most unseasonably fill with mistaken contempt, and others with an overweening empty aspiration, as though they had learnt some sublime mysteries.[15]

> Whenever one sees a man's written compositions – whether they be the laws of a legislator or anything else in any other form – these are not his most serious works, if it so be that the writer himself is serious: rather those works abide in the fairest region he possesses. If, however, these really are his serious efforts, and put into writing, it is not 'the gods' but mortal men who 'then of a truth themselves have utterly ruined his senses'.[16]

We must bear this discord in mind as we scrutinise the Platonic dialogue to discover how Socrates accomplished his pedagogic task.

One achievement is universally conceded to him: that by his questioning he leads his pupils to confess their ignorance and thus cuts through the roots of their dogmatism. This result, which indeed cannot be *forced* in any other way, discloses the significance of the dialogue as an instrument of instruction. The lecture, too, can stimulate spontaneous thinking, particularly in more mature students; but no matter what allure such stimulus may possess, it is not *irresistible*. Only persistent pressure to speak one's mind, to meet every counter-question, and to state the reasons for every assertion transforms the power of that allure into an irresistible compulsion. This art of *forcing* minds *to freedom* constitutes the first secret of the Socratic Method.

But only the first. For it does not take the pupil beyond the abandonment of his prejudices, the realisation of his not-knowing, this negative determinant of all genuine and certain knowledge.

Socrates, after this higher level of ignorance is reached, far from directing the discussion toward the metaphysical problems, blocks every attempt of his pupils to push straight on to them with the injunction that they had better first learn about the life of the weavers, the blacksmiths, the carters. In this pattern of the discussion we recognise the philosophical instinct for the only correct method: first to derive the general premises from the observed facts of everyday life, and thus to proceed from judgements of which we are sure to those that are less sure.

It is astonishing how little understood this simple guiding idea of method is even in our own day. Take, for example, the assertion that his use of the affairs of the workaday world as a point of departure exhibits merely the practical interest Socrates took in the moral jolting of his fellow citizens. No – had Socrates been concerned with natural philosophy rather than with ethics, he would still have introduced his ideas in the same way.

We arrive at no better understanding of the Socratic Method when we consider the way it works back from particulars to universals as a method of regressive inference, thereby identifying it with the inductive method. Though Aristotle praised him for it, Socrates was not the inventor of the inductive method. Rather, he pursued the path of abstraction, which employs reflection to lift the knowledge we already possess into consciousness. Had Aristotle been correct in his interpretation, we should not be surprised at the failure of Socrates' endeavours. For ethical principles cannot be derived from observed facts.

The truth is that in the execution of his design Socrates does fail. His sense of truth guides him surely through the introduction of the abstraction; but further on so many erroneous methodological ideas intrude that the success of the conversation is almost always frustrated.

In this process of separation from the particulars of experience and in his search for the more universal truths, Socrates concentrates his attention wholly on the general characteristics of concepts as we grasp them and devotes himself to the task of making these concepts explicit by definition. Without concepts, of course, there is no definite comprehension of general rational truths; but the elucidation of concepts and the discussion of their interrelations do not suffice to gain the content of the synthetic truths that are the true object of his quest.

What holds Socrates on his futile course is a mistake that comes to light only in Plato and gives his doctrine of ideas its ambivalent, half-mystic, half-logicising character. This doctrine assumes that concepts are images of the ideas that constitute ultimate reality. This is why the Socratic-Platonic dialogues see the summit of scientific knowledge in the elucidation of concepts.

It is not difficult for us to discern in retrospect the error that caused philosophy here to stray from the right path, and consequently hindered the elaboration of methods of abstraction requisite for scientific metaphysics. However, it would be beside the point to dwell on the shortcomings of a philosophy that for the first time made an attempt at critical self-analysis. Our present concern is not with its errors or with the incompleteness of its system but with its bold and sure beginnings that opened the road to philosophical truth.

Socrates was the first to combine with confidence in the ability of the human mind to recognise philosophical truth the conviction that this truth is not arrived at through occasional bright ideas or mechanical teaching but that only planned, unremitting, and consistent thinking leads us from darkness into its light. Therein lies

Socrates' greatness as a philosopher. His greatness as a pedagogue is based on another innovation: he made his pupils do their own thinking and introduced the interchange of ideas as a safeguard against self-deception.

In the light of this evaluation, the Socratic Method, for all its deficiencies, remains the only method for teaching philosophy. Conversely, all philosophical instruction is fruitless if it conflicts with Socrates' basic methodic requirements.

Of course, the development of philosophical knowledge had to free from its entanglement with Platonic mysticism the doctrine of reminiscence, the truth of which constitutes the real and most profound reason for the possibility of and necessity for the Socratic Method. This liberation was achieved after two thousand years by the critical philosophies of Kant and Fries. They carried the regressive method of abstraction to completion. Beyond this, they firmly secured the results of abstraction – which as basic principles do not admit of proof but as propositions must nevertheless be verified – by the method of *deduction*.

In the idea of this deduction – with which only Fries really succeeded – the doctrine of reminiscence experienced its resurrection. It is not too much to say that the Socratic-Platonic concept was thus transmuted from the prophetic/symbolic form, in which it had been confined by the two Greek sages, into the solidly welded and unshakably established form of a science.

Deduction, this master achievement of philosophy, is not easy to explain. I could not indicate its nature more succinctly than by saying that it is quite literally the instrumentality for carrying out the Socratic design to instruct the ignorant by compelling them to realise that they actually know what they did not know they knew.

★ ★ ★

Kant and Fries did not pursue the problem of instruction in philosophy beyond some incidental pedagogic observations of a general character. But, thanks to critical philosophy, philosophical science has made such progress in surmounting its inherent methodological difficulties that now the most urgent task of critical philosophy is the revival and furtherance of the Socratic Method, especially in its bearing on teaching. Must another two thousand years elapse before a kindred genius appears and rediscovers the ancient truth? Our science requires a continual succession of trained philosophers, at once independent and well schooled, to avert the danger that critical philosophy may either fall a victim of incomprehension or, though continuing in name, it yet may become petrified into dogmatism.

In view of the importance of this task, we shall do well to pause once more and scrutinise the whole of the difficulty we must face. The exposition of our problem has disclosed the profound relation between critical philosophy and the Socratic Method, on the basis of which we determine that the essence of the Socratic Method consists in freeing instruction from dogmatism; in other words, in excluding all didactic judgements from instruction. Now we are confronted with the full gravity of the pedagogic problem we are to solve. Consider the question: 'How is any instruction and therefore any teaching at all possible when every instructive judgement is forbidden?' Let us not attempt evasion by assuming that the requirement cannot possibly be meant to go to the extreme of prohibiting an occasional discreet helpful hint from teacher to student. No, there must be an honest choice: either dogmatism or following Socrates. The question then becomes all the more insistent: 'How is Socratic instruction possible?'

Here we come up against the basic problem of education, which in its general form points to the question: 'How is education at all possible?' If the end of education is rational self-determination, ie, a condition in which the individual does not allow his behaviour to be determined by outside influences, but judges and acts according to his own insight, the question arises: 'How can we affect a person by outside influences so that he will not permit himself to be affected by outside influences?' We must resolve this paradox or abandon the task of education.

The first thing to note is that in nature the human mind is always under external influences and, indeed, that the mind cannot develop without external stimulus. We then are confronted with the still broader question: 'Is self-determination compatible with the fact that in nature the mind is subject to external influence?'

It will help us to clarify our thinking if we distinguish between the two senses in which the term 'external influence' is used. It may mean external influence in general or an external determinant. Similarly, in teaching it may mean external stimulation of the mind or moulding the mind to the acceptance of outside judgements.

It is clearly no contradiction to hold both that the human mind finds within itself the cognitive source of philosophical truth and that insight into this truth is awakened in the mind by external stimuli. Indeed, the mind requires such external stimulation if the initial obscurity of philosophical truth is to grow into clear knowledge. Within the limits set by these conditions, instruction in philosophy is possible and even necessary if the development of the pupil is to be independent of mere chance.

Philosophical instruction fulfils its task when it systematically weakens the influences that obstruct the growth of philosophical comprehension and re-inforces those that promote it. Without going into the question of other relevant influences, let us keep firmly in mind the one that must be excluded unconditionally: the influence that may emanate from the instructor's assertions. If this influence is not eliminated, all labour is in vain. The instructor will have done everything possible to forestall the pupil's own judgement by offering him a ready-made judgement.

We are now arrived at a point from which we have a clear view both of the task of the Socratic Method and of the possibility of fulfilling it. The rest must be left to the experiment and the degree of conviction it may carry.

★ ★ ★

But it would be underrating the difficulty presented not to consider what the experiment must call for if from its outcome we are to decide whether or not our goal is attainable. Although I have been taxing your patience for some time, I should render a poor service to our cause, and thus to you too, if I did not engage your attention a while longer to consider the procedure of such an experiment.

There is a danger inherent in the nature of an exacting enterprise, whose success has met with a little recognition, and it is this: the participants in it, once they become involved in its mounting difficulties and unexpected distractions, will repent of their good intentions or at least begin to think of ways of modifying the method to make it easier. This tendency, springing from purely subjective discomfort, is likely to distort or completely frustrate the object of the undertaking. It is therefore advisable, lest expectations be disappointed, to envisage in advance as clearly as possible the manifold difficulties that will surely arise and, with due appreciation of these difficulties, to set down what will be required of teachers and students.

We must bear in mind that instruction in philosophy is not concerned with heaping solution on solution, nor indeed with establishing results, but solely with learning the method of reaching solutions. If we do this, we shall observe at once that the teacher's proper role cannot be that of a guide keeping his party from wrong paths and accidents. Nor yet is he a guide going in the lead while his party simply follow in the expectation that this will prepare them to find the same path later on by themselves. On the contrary, the essential thing is the skill with which the teacher puts the pupils on their own responsibility at the very beginning by teaching them to go by themselves – although they would not on that account go alone – and by so developing this independence that one day they might be able to venture forth alone, self-guidance having replaced the teacher's supervision.

As to the observations I am about to make, I must beg to be allowed to offer incidental examples from my own long experience as a teacher of philosophy, for unfortunately the experiences of others are not at my disposal.

Let me take up first the requirements imposed on the teacher and then go on to those placed on a pupil. Once a student of mine, endeavouring to reproduce a Socratically conducted exercise, presented a version in which he puts the replies now into the teacher's mouth, now into the pupil's. Only my astonished question, 'Have you ever heard me say 'yes' or 'no'?' stopped him short. Thrasymachus saw the point more clearly; in Plato's *Republic* he calls out to Socrates: 'Ye gods! ... I knew it ... that you would refuse and do anything rather than answer.'[17] The teacher who follows the Socratic model does not answer. Neither does he question. More precisely, he puts no philosophical questions, and when such questions are addressed to him, he under no circumstances gives the answer sought. Does he then remain silent? We shall see. During such a session we may often hear the despairing appeal to the teacher: 'I don't know what it is you want!' Whereupon the teacher replies: 'I? I want nothing at all.' This certainly does not convey the desired information. What is it, then, that the teacher actually does? He sets the interplay of question and answer going between the students, perhaps by the introductory remark: 'Has anyone a question?'

Now, everyone will realise that, as Kant said, 'to know what questions may reasonably be asked is already a great and necessary proof of sagacity and insight.'[18] What about foolish questions, or what if there are no questions at all? Suppose nobody answers?

You see, at the very beginning the difficulty presents itself of getting the students to the point of spontaneous activity, and with it arises the temptation for the teacher to pay out a clue like Ariadne's thread. But the teacher must be firm from the beginning, and especially at the beginning. If a student approaches philosophy without having a single question to put to it, what can we expect in the way of his capacity to persevere in exploring its complex and profound problems?

What should the teacher do if there are no questions? He should wait – until questions come. At most, he should request that in future, to save time, questions be thought over in advance. But he should not, just to save time, spare the students the effort of formulating their own questions. If he does, he may temper their impatience for the moment, but only at the cost of nipping in the bud the philosophical impatience we seek to awaken.

Once questions start coming – one by one, hesitantly, good ones and foolish ones – how does the teacher receive them, how does he handle them? He now seems to have it easy since the rule of Socratic Method forbids his answering them. He submits the questions to discussion.

All of them? The appropriate and the inappropriate?

By no means. He ignores all questions uttered in too low a voice. Likewise those that are phrased incoherently. How can difficult ideas be grasped when they are expressed in mutilated language?

Thanks to the extraordinary instruction in the mother tongue given in our schools, over half the questions are thus eliminated. [*Nelson is referring to German schools. The reader may judge to what degree this criticism also applies to schools in the United States and England.* eds] As for the rest, many are confused or vague. Sometimes clarification comes with the counter-question: 'Just what do you mean by that?' But very often this will not work because the speaker does not know what he means himself. The work of the discussion group thus tends automatically either to take up the clear simple questions or to clear up unclear, vague ones first.

We are not so fortunate in the problems of philosophy as we are in the problems of mathematics, which, as Hilbert says, fairly calls to us 'Here I am, find the solution!' The philosophical problem is wrapped in obscurity. To be able to come to grips with it by framing clear-cut, searching questions demands many trials and much effort. It will therefore scarcely surprise you to learn that a semester's work in a seminar in ethics yielded nothing except agreement on the fact that the initial question was incongruous. The question was, 'Is it not stupid to act morally?'

Of course, the instructor will not submit every incongruous question to such protracted examination. He will seek to advance the discussion through his own appraisal of the questions. But he will do no more than allow a certain question to come to the fore because it is instructive in itself or because threshing it out will bring to light typical errors. And he will do this by some such expedient as following the question up with the query: 'Who understood what was said just now?' This contains no indication of the relevance or irrelevance of the question; it is merely an invitation to consider it, to extract its meaning by intensive cross-examination.

What is his policy as regards the answers? How are they handled? They are treated like the questions. Unintelligible answers are ignored in order to teach the students to meet the requirements of scientific speech. Answers, too, are probed through such questions as:

> What has this answer to do with our question?
> Which word do you wish to emphasise?
> Who has been following?
> Do you still know what you said a few moments ago?
> What question are we talking about?

The simpler these questions, the more flustered the students become. Then, if a fellow student takes pity on his colleague's distress and comes to his aid with the explanation, 'He surely wanted to say ....', this helpful gesture is unfeelingly cut short with the request to let the art of mind-reading alone and cultivate instead the modest art of saying what one actually wants to say.

By this time you will have gathered that the investigations run a far from even course. Questions and answers tumble over one another. Some of the students understand the development and some do not. The latter cut in with groping questions, trying to re-establish contact, but the others will not be stopped from going ahead. They disregard the interruptions. New questions crop up, wider of the mark. Here and there a debater falls silent; then whole groups. Meanwhile, the agitation continues, and questions become constantly more pointless. Even those who were originally sure of their ground become confused. They, too, lose the thread and do not know how to find it again. Finally, nobody knows where the discussion is headed.

The bewilderment famed in the Socratic circle closes in. Everyone is at his wit's end. What had been certain at the outset has become uncertain. The students, instead of clarifying their own conceptions, now feel as though they have been robbed of their capacity to make anything clear by thinking.

And does the teacher tolerate this too?

'I consider,' says Meno to his teacher Socrates, in the dialogue bearing his name, 'that both in appearance and in other respects you are extremely like the flat torpedo fish; for it benumbs anyone who approaches and touches it. . . . For in truth I feel my soul and my tongue quite benumbed and I am at a loss what answer to give you.'[19]

When Socrates replies, 'It is from being in more doubt than anyone else that I cause doubts in others,' Meno counters with the celebrated question: 'Why, on what lines will you look, Socrates, for a thing of whose nature you know nothing at all?' And this draws from Socrates the more celebrated answer: 'Because the soul should be able to recollect all that she knew before.'[20] We all know that these words are an echo of the Platonic doctrine of ideas, which the historic Socrates did not teach. Yet there is in them the Socratic spirit, the stout spirit of reason's self-confidence, its reverence for its own self-sufficient strength. This strength gives Socrates the composure that permits him to let the seekers after truth go astray and stumble. More than that, it gives him the courage to send them astray in order to test their convictions, to separate knowledge simply taken over from the truth that slowly attains clarity in us through our own reflection. He is unafraid of the confession of not knowing; indeed, he even induces it. In this he is guided by an attitude of thinking so far from sceptical that he regards this admission as the first step toward deeper knowledge. 'He does not think he knows ... and is he not better off in respect of the matter which he did not know?' he says of the slave to whom he gives instruction in mathematics. 'For now he will push on in the search gladly, as lacking knowledge.'[21]

To Socrates the test of whether a man loves wisdom is whether he welcomes his ignorance in order to attain to better knowledge. The slave in the *Meno* does this and goes on with the task. Many, however, slacken and tire of the effort when they find their knowledge belittled, when they find that their first few unaided steps do not get them far. The teacher of philosophy who lacks the courage to put his pupils to the test of perplexity and discouragement not only deprives them of the opportunity to develop the endurance needed for research but also deludes them concerning their capabilities and makes them dishonest with themselves.

Now we can discern one of the sources of error that provoke the familiar unjust criticisms of the Socratic Method. This method is charged with a defect which it merely reveals and which it must reveal to prepare the ground on which alone the continuation of serious work is possible. It simply uncovers the harm that has been done to men's minds by dogmatic teaching.

Is it a fault of the Socratic Method that it must take time for such elementary matters as ascertaining what question is being discussed or determining what the speaker intended to say about it? It is easy for dogmatic instruction to soar into higher regions. Indifferent to self-understanding, it purchases its illusory success at the cost of more and more deeply rooted dishonesty. It is not surprising, then, that the Socratic Method is compelled to fight a desperate battle for integrity of thought and speech before it can turn to larger tasks. It must also suffer the additional reproach of being unphilosophical enough to orient itself by means of examples and facts.

The only way one can learn to recognise and avoid the pitfalls of reflection is to become acquainted with them in *application*, even at the risk of gaining wisdom only by sad experience. It is useless to preface philosophising proper with an introductory course in logic in the hope of thus saving the novice from the risk of taking the wrong path. Knowledge of the principles of logic and the rules of the syllogism, even the ability to illustrate every fallacy by examples, remains after all an art *in abstracto*. An individual is far from learning to think logically even though he has learned to conclude by all the syllogistic rules that Caius is mortal. The test of one's own conclusions and their subjection to the rules of logic is the province of one's faculty of judgement, not at all the province of logic. The faculty of judgement, said Kant, being the power of rightly employing given rules, 'must belong to the learner himself; and in the absence of such a natural gift no rule that maybe prescribed to him for this purpose can ensure against misuse.'[22] If, therefore, this natural gift is weak, it must be strengthened. But it can be strengthened only by exercise.

Thus, after our instructor breaks the spell of numbness by calling for a return to the original question, and the students trace their way back to the point from which they started, each must, by critical examination of every one of his steps, study the sources of error and work out for himself his own school of logic. Rules of logic derived from personal experience retain a living relation with the judgements they are to govern. Furthermore, the fact that dialectics, though indispensable, is introduced as an auxiliary only prevents attaching an exaggerated value to it in the manner of scholasticism, to which the most trivial metaphysical problem served for the exercise of logical ingenuity. Segregation of the philosophical disciplines with a view to reducing the difficulties of instruction by separate treatment would be worse than a waste of time. Other ways will have to be found to satisfy the pedagogic maxim that our requirements of the pupil should become progressively more stringent.

This question, if examined carefully, presents no further difficulties for us. If there is such a thing as a research method for philosophy, its essential element must consist of practical directives for the step-by-step solution of problems. It is therefore simply a question of letting the student himself follow the path of the regressive method. The first step, obviously, is to have him secure a firm footing in experience – which is harder to do than an outsider might think. For your adept in philosophy scorns nothing so much as using his intelligence concretely in forming judgements on real facts, an operation that obliges him to remember those lowly instruments of cognition, his five senses. Ask anyone at a philosophy seminar, 'What do you see on the blackboard?' and – depend on it – he will look at the floor. Upon your repeating, 'What do you see *on the blackboard*?' he will finally wrench out a sentence that begins with 'If' and demonstrates that for him the world of facts does not exist.

He shows the same disdain for reality when asked to give an example. Forthwith he goes off into a world of fantasy or, if forced to stay on this planet, he at least makes off to the sea or into the desert, so that one wonders whether being attacked by lions and saved from drowning are typical experiences among the acquaintances of a philosopher. The 'if' sentences, the far-fetched examples, and the premature desire for definitions characterise not the ingenious beginner but rather the philosophically indoctrinated dilettante. And it is always he, with his pseudo-wisdom, who disturbs the quiet and simple progress of an investigation.

I recall a seminar in logic, in which the desire to start from general definitions – under the impression that otherwise the concepts being discussed could not be employed – caused much fruitless trouble. Despite my warning, the group stuck to the opening question: 'What is a concept?'

It was not long before a casual reference to the concept 'lamp' as an example was followed by the appearance of the 'lamp in general' provided with all the essential characteristics of all particular lamps. The students waxed warm in vehement dispute regarding the proof of the existence of this lamp furnished with all the essential features of all particular lamps. My diffident question, whether the lamp-in-general was fed with gas, electricity or kerosene, went unanswered as unworthy of philosophical debate until, hours later, the resumption of this very question of the source of energy forced the negation of the existence of the lamp-in-general. That is to say, the disputants discovered that different illuminants for one and the same lamp, be it ever so general, were mutually exclusive. Thus, starting with practical application, they had unexpectedly found the law of contradiction by the regressive method. But to define the concept of a concept had proved a vain endeavour, just as in the Socratic circle the definitions nearly always miscarried.

Are we justified, however, in assuming that the cause of such failures lies in conditions unconnected with the Socratic Method itself? Does not this method perhaps suffer from an inherent limitation that makes the solution of deeper problems impossible?

Before coming to a final decision on this point, we must consider one more factor that creates difficulty in the employment of the Socratic Method. Though intimately associated with the latter, it lies outside it, yet demands consideration before we can set the limits of the method itself.

The significance of the Socratic Dialogue has been sought in the assumption that deliberating with others makes us more easily cognisant of truth than silent reflection. Obviously, there is much soundness in this view. Yet many a person may be moved to doubt this praise after he has listened to the hodgepodge of questions and answers at a philosophical debate and noted the absence, despite the outward discipline, of the tranquillity that belongs to reflection. It is inevitable that what is said by one participant may prove disturbing to another, whether he feels himself placed in a dependent position by intelligent remarks or is distracted by poor ones. It is inevitable that collaboration should progressively become a trial of nerves, made more difficult by increasing demands on personal tact and tolerance.

To a great extent these disturbances can be obviated by an instructor who, for instance, will ignore the innumerable senseless answers, cast doubt on the right ones with Socratic irony, or ease nervous unrest with some understanding word. But his power to restore harmony to the play of ideas is limited unless the others are willing to pursue the common task with determination.

It should be admitted that many disturbances are unavoidable because of the students' imperfect understanding; but the obstacles I have in mind do not lie in the intellectual sphere and for that reason even the most skilful teacher finds them an insurmountable barrier. He can enforce intellectual discipline only if the students are possessed of a disciplined will. This may sound strange but it is a fact that one becomes a philosopher, not by virtue of intellectual gifts but by the exercise of will.

True, philosophising demands considerable power of intellect. But who will exercise it? Surely not the man who relies merely on his intellectual power. As he delves more deeply into his studies and his difficulties multiply, he will without fail weaken. Because of his intelligence he will recognise these difficulties, even see them very clearly. But the elasticity required to face a problem again and again, to stay with it until it is solved, and not to succumb to disintegrating doubt – this elasticity is achieved only through the power of an iron will, a power of which the entertaining ingenuity of the mere sophist knows nothing. In the end, his intellectual fireworks are as sterile for science as the intellectual dullness that shrinks back at the first obstacle. It is no accident that the investigators whom the history of philosophy records as having made the most decisive advances in dialectics were at the same time philosophers in the original meaning of the word. Only because they loved wisdom were they able to take upon themselves the 'many preliminary subjects it entails and [so] much labour', as Plato says in a letter that continues:

> For on hearing this, if the pupil be truly philosophical, in sympathy with the subject and worthy of it, because divinely gifted, he believes that he has been shown a marvellous pathway and that he must brace himself at once to follow it, and that life will not be worth living if he does otherwise. ...
>
> Those, on the other hand, who are in reality not philosophical, but superficially tinged with opinions – like men whose bodies are sunburnt on the surface – when they see how many studies are required and how great labour, and how the disciplined mode of daily life is that which benefits the subject, they deem it difficult or impossible for themselves.[23]

That is the clear and most definite characteristic of

> those who are luxurious and incapable of enduring labour, since [the test] prevents any of them from ever casting the blame on his instructor instead of on himself and his own inability to pursue all the studies which are necessary to his subject.[23]
>
> In one word, neither receptivity nor memory will ever produce knowledge in him who has no affinity with the object, since it does not germinate to start with in alien states of mind.[24]

We, in common with Plato, require of the philosopher that he strengthen his will power, but it is impossible to achieve this as a by-product in the course of philosophical instruction. The student's willpower must be the fruit of his prior education. It is the instructor's duty to make no concession on maintaining the rigorous and indispensable demands on the will; indeed, he must do so out of respect for the students themselves. If, for the want of requisite firmness, he allows himself to be persuaded to relax his stand, or if he does so of his own accord to hold his following, he will have betrayed his philosophical goal. He has no alternative; he must insist on his demands or give up the task. Everything else is abject compromise.

Of course, the student should know the details of the demands to be made on his will. They constitute the minimum required for examining ideas in a group. This means, first, the communication of thoughts, not of acquired fragments of knowledge, not even the knowledge of other people's thoughts. It means, further, the use of clear, unambiguous language. Only the compulsion to communicate provides a means of testing the definiteness and clarity of one's own conceptions. Here, protesting that one has the right feeling but cannot express it will not avail. Feeling is indeed the first and best guide on the path to truth, but it is often the protector of prejudice. In a scientific matter, therefore, feeling must be interpreted so that it may be evaluated in accordance with concepts and ordered logic. Moreover, our investigation demands the communication of ideas in distinctly audible and generally comprehensible speech, free from ambiguities. A technical terminology is not only unnecessary for philosophising but is actually detrimental to its steady progress. It imparts to metaphysical matters, abstract and difficult in any case, the appearance of an esoteric science which only superior minds are qualified to penetrate. It prevents us from considering the conclusions of unprejudiced judgement, which we have seen to be the starting point of meaningful philosophising. Unprejudiced judgement, in its operation, relies on concepts that we have, not on artificial reflections, and it makes its conclusions understood by strict adherence to current linguistic usage.

In order to grasp those concepts clearly it is necessary to isolate them. By the process of abstraction it is possible to separate them from other ideas, to reduce them gradually to their elements, and through such analyses to advance to basic concepts. By holding fast to existing concepts, the philosopher guards himself against peopling his future system with the products of mere speculation and with fantastic brain-children. For, if he does not consult unprejudiced judgement, he will allow himself to be lured into forming philosophical concepts by the arbitrary combination of specific characteristics, without any assurance that objects corresponding to his constructions actually exist. Only the use of the same vocabulary still connects him with the critical philosopher. He denotes his artificial concept by the same word the critical philosopher uses to denote his real concept, although, to be sure, he uses this word in a different sense. He says 'I' and means 'cosmic reason'. He says 'God' and means 'peace of mind'. He says 'state' and means 'power subject to no law'. He says 'marriage' and means 'indissoluble communion of love'. He says 'space' and means 'the labyrinth of the ear'. His language is full of artificial meanings. Although it is not apparent, his is actually a technical language; and because this is so, the situation is far more dangerous than it would be if the philosopher indicated the special sense of his language by coining specific new terms. For the sameness of the words tricks the unwary into associating their own familiar concepts with them, and misunderstanding results. What is more pernicious, this artificial language tempts its own creator to the covert use of the same words in different meanings, and by such a shift of concepts he produces sham proofs. In this abuse of purely verbal definitions we encounter one of the most prevalent and profound of dialectical errors, an error that is rendered more difficult to track down by the fact that the shift of concepts cannot be discovered simply by calling on intuition. However, it betrays itself through its consequences, through the curious phenomenon that with the help of the same verbal definition the pseudo-proof presented can be confronted with a contrary proof that has the same air of validity.

The most celebrated and memorable instance of such antitheses is found in the antinomies that Kant discovered and solved. Kant said of these classic examples of contradiction that they were the most beneficent aberration in the history of reason because they furnished the incentive to investigate the cause of the illusion and to reconcile reason to itself. This remark is applicable to every instance of such dialectical conflict.

It will seem, perhaps, that in these last considerations we have strayed somewhat from our subject; the requirement that the student use distinctly audible and generally comprehensible language. But, as a matter of fact, we have secured a deeper understanding of the significance of that requirement.

After all we have said, what is it that we gain with this demand on the pupil? Only those who, by using comprehensible language, adhere to the concepts we have and become practised in discussing them will sharpen their critical sense for every arbitrary definition and for every sham proof adroitly derived from such verbal definition. If the requirement of simple and clear language is observed, it is possible, in Socratic teaching, merely by writing the theses of two mutually contradictory doctrines on the blackboard, to focus attention on the verbal definition underlying them, disclose its abuse, and thereby overthrow both doctrinal opinions. The success of such a dialectical performance is achieved – and this is its significant feature – not by flashes of inspiration but methodically, ie, through a step-by-step search for the hidden premise at the bottom of the contradictory judgements. This method will succeed if the student, struck with suspicion at such a sophism, attends closely to the meaning of the words, for these words, when used in an inartificial sense, put him on the track of the error.

Do not misunderstand me. I do not advocate the point of view that so-called common sense and its language can satisfy the demands of scientific philosophising. Nor is it my purpose, in dwelling on simple elementary conditions seemingly easy to fulfil, to veil the fact that the pursuit of philosophising requires rigorous training in the art of abstraction, one difficult to master. My point is this: We cannot with impunity skip the first steps in the development of this art. Abstraction must have something to abstract from. The immediate and tangible material of philosophy is language which presents concepts through words. In its wealth, supplied from many sources, reason dwells concealed. Reflection discloses this rational knowledge by separating it from intuitive notions.

Just as Socrates took pains to question locksmiths and blacksmiths and made their activities the first subject of discussion with his pupils, so every philosopher ought to start out with the vernacular and develop the language of his abstract science from its pure elements.

I am now done with the requirements that apply to the students. Their difficulty lies not in the fulfilment of details but in the observance of the whole. I said earlier that the working agreement with the students requires of them nothing but the communication of their ideas. You will understand if I now express the same demand in another form: it requires of the students submission to the method of philosophising, for it is the sole aim of Socratic instruction to enable the students to judge for themselves their observance of the agreement.

* * *

Our examination of the Socratic Method is nearing its conclusion. Now that we have discussed the difficulties of its application, there remains only one query: May not the reason for the unfavourable reception of the method lie, in part at least, within itself? Is there not perhaps some limitation inherent in it that restricts its usefulness?

One singular fact, more than any other, is calculated to make us consider this doubt seriously. Fries, the one man who actually completed critical philosophy and restored the Socratic-Platonic doctrine of reminiscence and the self-certainty of intelligence, Fries, the most genuine of all Socrateans, gave the Socratic Method only qualified recognition because he considered it inadequate for achieving complete self-examination of the intellect. He acknowledged its capacity to guide the novice in the early stages; he even demanded emphatically that all instruction on philosophy follow the spirit of the Socratic Method, the essence of which, he held, lay not in its use of dialogue but in its 'starting from the common things of everyday life and only then going on from these to scientific views'.[25] 'But as soon as higher truths, further removed from intuition and everyday experience, are involved',[26] Fries did not approve of letting the students find these truths by themselves. 'Here the instructor must employ a language moulded upon subtle abstractions, of which the student does not yet have complete command, and to which he must be educated by instruction'.[27]

In Fries's own words, this lecture method of instruction 'step by step invites cooperative thinking'.[28] An illustration of it is given in his didactic novel, *Julius and Evagoras*. And indeed it is not a form of Socratic instruction.

I should not think of choosing a really successful dialogue of Plato's – were there such – as subject matter for a philosophy seminar as it would forestall the creative thinking of students, but there is nothing in *Julius and Evagoras* to preclude its use for such a purpose. For the development of abstract ideas which it presents to the reader does indeed 'invite' critical verification by the students, as Fries desires. However, though otherwise exemplary, it offers no assurance that the students will accept the invitation or, if made to stand on their own feet, that they will master such difficulties as they may encounter on their way. Have your students study the fine and instructive chapter on 'The Sources of Certainty', and I stand ready to demonstrate in a Socratic discussion that those students will lack everything that would enable them to defend what they have learned. The key to this riddle is to be found in Goethe's words: 'One sees only what one already knows.'

It is futile to lay a sound, clear, and well-grounded theory before the students; futile though they respond to the invitation to follow in their thinking. It is even useless to point out to them the difficulties they would have to overcome in order to work out such results independently. If they are to become independent masters of philosophical theory, it is imperative that they go beyond the mere learning of problems and their difficulties; they must wrestle with them in constant practical application so that, through dealing with them day by day, they may learn to overcome them with all their snares and pitfalls and diversities of form. However, the instructor's lecture that Fries would have delivered 'in language moulded upon subtle abstractions', just because of its definiteness and clarity, will obscure the difficulties that hamper the development of this very lucidity of thought and verbal precision. The outcome will be that in the end only those already expert in Socratic thinking will assimilate the philosophical substance and appreciate the soundness and originality of the exposition.

Fries underrated the Socratic Method because, for one thing, he did not and could not find the Socratic Method in the method of Socrates, and he considered this fact as confirming his opinion of the inadequacy of the Socratic Method. Another reason – and the more profound, I think – lay in the particular character of Fries's genius. He combined with a sense of truth unparalleled in the history of philosophy a linguistic gift that produced with the assurance of a somnambulist the words that were appropriate to a philosophical idea. A man with a mind so superior, rich and free will always find it difficult to maintain close contact with the minds of less independent thinkers. He is prone to overlook the danger of dogmatism that threatens the more dependent mind even when the instructor's lecture has reached the highest degree of lucidity and exactitude of expression. A man of such superiority can become a leader of generations of men. But this is contingent on the appearance of teachers who will find the key to his language by resorting to the maieutic services[29] of the Socratic Method, instituting the laborious and protracted exercises that must not frighten away those who plan to dedicate themselves to philosophy.

I maintain that this art has no limitations. I have seen a Socratic seminar not only deal successfully with such an abstract subject as the philosophy of law but even proceed to the construction of its system.

This is claiming a good deal, you will say. Well, I have enough Socratic irony to acknowledge the awkwardness of my position, which, incidentally, I admitted in the opening sentence of my address. For when all is said and done, no one will be won over to the cause I am pleading here except by the evidence of the experiment, that is, through his own experience.

But let us look about us: Can we not find some sufficiently simple and well-known control experiment that permits a valid conclusion on the question at issue? What sort of experiment might that be? If non-Socratically conducted instruction could accomplish the designated end in philosophy, such a procedure should succeed all the more readily in a science that does not have to struggle with the particular difficulties of philosophical knowledge – a science in which, on the contrary, everything from first to last becomes absolutely and completely clear even when set forth in a dogmatic lecture.

If we inquire whether there is such a science and, if so, whether it has a place among the subjects of instruction in our schools and universities, we find that such a science actually does exist. Mathematics satisfies both conditions. 'We are in possession', said a classic French mathematician. The relevant experiment is thus available, and we need only consider its outcome with an unprejudiced mind.

What does it teach? Just among ourselves and without glossing over anything or blaming anyone, we teachers might as well confess to what is a public secret: on the whole the result is negative. We all know from personal experience that diligent and even gifted students in our secondary schools and colleges, if seriously put to the test, are not sure of even the rudiments of mathematics and discover their own ignorance.

Our experiment therefore points to the conclusion I spoke of; as a matter of fact, there is no escaping it. Suppose someone were to say there is no such thing as understanding, regardless of the kind of instruction. That is arguable, but not for us as pedagogues. We start from the assumption that meaningful instruction is possible. And then we must come to the conclusion that, if there is any assurance that a subject can be understood, Socratic instruction offers such assurance. And with that we have found more than we sought, for this conclusion applies not only to philosophy but to every subject that involves comprehension.

An experiment conducted by history itself on a grand scale confirms the fact that the pedagogic inadequacy in the field of mathematics is not due merely to incompetent teachers but must have a more fundamental cause; or, to put it differently, that even the best mathematics instruction, if it follows the dogmatic method, cannot, despite all its clearness, bring about thorough understanding. This experiment deserves the attention of everyone interested in the teaching of mathematics.

The basic principles of calculus (nowadays included in the curricula of some of our high schools) became the secure and acknowledged possession of science only in the mid- nineteenth century, when they were first established with clarity and exactitude. Although the most important results had been a matter of general knowledge ever since Newton and Leibniz, their foundations remained in dispute. Endlessly repeated attempts at elucidation only resulted in new obscurities and paradoxes. Considering the state of this branch of mathematics at that time, Berkeley was not unjustified when he undertook to prove that in the unintelligibility of its theories it was not one whit behind the dogmas and mysteries of theology.[30] We know today that those riddles were solvable, that, thanks to the work of Cauchy and Weierstrass, they have been solved, and that this branch of mathematics is susceptible of the same clarity and lucidity of structure as elementary geometry. Here, too, everything becomes evident as soon as attention is focused on the decisive point. But it is precisely this that is hard to achieve, an art each student must acquire by his own efforts.

To demonstrate how true this is, I shall mention two especially noteworthy facts. The first is this: Newton's treatise, widely known and celebrated since its appearance, not only expounds the decisive point of view established by Cauchy and Weierstrass but formulates it with a clarity, precision and succinctness that would satisfy the most exacting requirements contemporary science could lay down. Moreover, it contains an explicit warning against that very misunderstanding which, as we now know, kept succeeding generations of mathematicians so completely in bondage that their minds remained closed to the emphatic '*Cave!*' of the classic passage in Newton's work,[31] familiar to all of them.

The second, the complement, as it were, of the first, is that, even after Weierstrass and after the argument had at long last been settled, it was possible to revive it only among dilettanti, whom we shall always have with us, but even under the leadership of a man of research as distinguished for his work on the theory of functions as Paul du Bois-Reymond. In his own words, his 'solution is that it remains and will remain a riddle'.[32]

There is an impressive warning in this instance of the disparity between the objective lucidity and systematic completeness of a scientific theory, on the one hand, and any pedagogic assurance that it will be understood, on the other. It is precisely the man with a philosophical turn of mind who is unwilling, in mathematics as elsewhere, simply to accept a result; he philosophises about it, ie, he strives to understand its fundamentals and bring it into harmony with the rest of his knowledge. But it is just he who is sure to fail unless he is one of the few who find their way to clarity by their own efforts. We thus discover that even mathematics, instead of remaining the unassailable standard and model that might help philosophy, is drawn along by it into the whirlpool of confusion.

Herewith, I believe, I have also answered the weightiest comment I know on the value of the Socratic Method in teaching mathematics. It comes from no less a man than Weierstrass. He devoted a special essay to the Socratic Method,[33] an indication of the esteem and comprehension this profound mathematician and pedagogue had for our subject. His detailed argument is proof of this. He demonstrated the basic practicability of the Socratic Method in philosophy and pure mathematics, in contradistinction to the empirical sciences. That he nevertheless rated it as of little value for use in the school was due, for one thing, to the fact that he considered insurmountable the external difficulties which undeniably exist, and which I have dwelt on extensively. For another, he was obviously partial to the coherent lecture with its large perspectives and architectonic beauty of structure, a partiality easily understandable in a scientist of his genius. Still, he admitted that such a lecture 'presupposes students of rather more mature intelligence, if it is to be effective'. Since, however, it was also his opinion that 'the Socratic Method, carried out in its true spirit, ... is less suitable for boys than for more mature youths', one is impelled to ask (but in vain) how the maturity of mind can develop that will assure success to a non-Socratic mode of instruction.

★ ★ ★

What maturity of mind our students must have if they are to surpass Paul du Bois-Reymond, the pupil of Weierstrass, and Euler, the pupil of Newton, in depth of understanding!

Our findings might lead us to pessimism. But, if we view the matter rightly, we are not yet finished. What we have found indicates the way we can remove the cause of this lamentable state of affairs, which itself can hardly be regarded pessimistically enough.

The way lies in mathematics. It is within the power of the mathematicians to end the scandal that not only has completely undermined the authority of philosophy but also threatens mathematics itself with the loss of the prestige that, thanks to its powerful position in education, it has until now maintained in the intellectual life of mankind. In view of the deplorable situation in which the cause of the Socratic Method finds itself, help can come only through a science that combines the several advantages I have discussed, advantages that only mathematics has and that assure it a head start which philosophy can never overcome by its own efforts.

The character and repute of mathematics as a science still stand quite firm. In the long run, the evidence of its results cannot be obscured by any teaching, however wretched, and it will always offer a means of orientation though all else be plunged into darkness and confusion. I therefore appeal to the mathematicians. May they become aware of the spiritual power they hold and of their consequent mission of leadership in the fields of science and education. Philosophy cannot now assume the role, originally hers, of guardian of the intellectual values whose fate is bound up with that of the Socratic Method. Having disowned her stepchild and thus deprived herself of its vitalising and rejuvenating influence, philosophy has become so infirm that she must now beg of her sister science asylum and aid for her cast-off daughter.

Though I said at the beginning that a sense of chivalry has made me champion of the disdained one, I am nevertheless far from blind to my powerlessness. I can fulfil this command of chivalry only by commending my protégée to the care of mathematics – confident that the outcast will be nurtured by it and grow vigorously until, her strength renewed, she returns to her own home and there establishes law and order, thus requiting with good the evil done her.

Appendix

A Midwifery for Men

Theætetus. I can assure you, Socrates, that I have tried very often to answer your questions; but I can neither persuade myself that I have any answer to give, nor hear of anyone who answers as you would have him. I cannot shake off a feeling of anxiety.

Socrates. These are the pangs of labour, my dear Theætetus; you have something within you which you are bringing to birth.

Theæt. I do not know, Socrates; I only say what I feel.

Soc. And did you never hear, simpleton, that I am the son of a midwife, brave and burly, whose name was Phænarete?

Theæt. Yes, I have.

Soc. And that I myself practise midwifery?

Theæt. No, never.

Soc. Let me tell you that I do, my friend; but you must not reveal the secret, as the world in general has not found me out; and therefore they only say of me, that I am the strangest of mortals, and drive men to their wits' end. Did you ever hear that too?

Theæt. Yes.

Soc. Shall I tell you the reason?

Theæt. By all means.

Soc. Bear in mind the whole business of the midwives, and then you will see my meaning better. By the use of potions and incantations they are able to arouse the pangs and to soothe them at will; they can make those bear who have a difficulty in bearing, and if they think fit, they can smother the embryo in the womb.

Theæt. They can.

Soc. Did you ever remark that they are also most cunning matchmakers, and have a thorough knowledge of what unions are likely to produce a brave brood?

Theæt. No never.

Soc. Then let me tell you that this is their greatest pride, more than cutting the umbilical cord. And if you reflect, you will see what the same art which cultivates and gathers in the fruits of the earth, will be most likely to know in what soils the several plants or seeds should be deposited.

Theæt. Yes, the same art.

Soc. And do you suppose that with women the case is otherwise?

Theæt. I should think not.

Soc. Certainly not, but midwives are respectable women and have a character to lose, and they avoid this department of their profession, because they are afraid of being called procuresses, which is a name given to those who join together man and woman in an unlawful and unscientific way; and yet the true midwife is also the true and only matchmaker.

Theæt. Clearly.

Soc. Such are the midwives, whose task is a very important one, but not so important as mine; for women do not bring into the world at one time real children, and at another time counterfeits which are with difficulty distinguished from them; if they did, then the discernment of the true and false birth would be the crowning achievement of the art of midwifery – you would think so?

Theætetus. Indeed I should.

Soc. Well, my art of midwifery is in most respects like theirs; but differs in that I attend men and not women, and I look after souls when they are in labour, and not after their bodies; and the triumph of my art is in thoroughly examining whether the thought which the mind of the young man is bringing to birth, is a false idol or a noble and true spirit.

And like midwives, I am barren, and the reproach which is often made against me, that I ask questions of others and have not the wit to answer them myself, is very just; the reason is, that the god compels me to be a midwife, but forbids me to bring forth.

And therefore I am not myself at all wise, nor have I anything to show which is the invention or birth of my own soul, but those who converse with me profit. Some of them appear dull enough at first, but afterwards, as our acquaintance ripens, if the god is gracious to them, they all make astonishing progress; and this in the opinion of others as well as their own.

It is quite clear that they had never learned anything from me; the many fine discoveries to which they cling are of their own making. But to me and the god they owe their delivery. And the proof of my words is, that many of them in their ignorance, either in their self-conceit despising me, or falling under the influence of others, have gone away too soon; and have not only lost the children of whom I had previously delivered them by an ill bringing up, but have stifled whatever else they had in them by evil communications, being fonder of lies and shams than of the truth; and they have at last ended by seeing themselves, as others see them, to be great fools. Dire are the pangs which my art is able to arouse and to allay in those who consort with me, just like the pangs of women in childbirth; night and day they are full of perplexity and travail which is even worse than that of the women.

So much of them. And there are others, Theætetus, who come to me apparently having nothing in them, and as I know that they have no need of my art, I coax them into marrying some one, and by the grace of God I can generally tell who is likely to do them good. Many of them I have given away to Prodicus, and many to other inspired sages.

I tell you this long story, friend Theætetus, because I suspect, as indeed you seem to think yourself, that you are in labour – great with some conception. Come then to me, who am a midwife's son and myself a midwife, and try to answer the questions which I will ask you. And if I abstract and expose your first-born, because I discover upon inspection that the conception which you have formed is a vain shadow, do not quarrel with me on that account, as the manner of women is when their first children are taken from them. For I have actually known some who were ready to bite me when I deprived them of a darling folly; they did not perceive that I acted from good will, not knowing that no god is the enemy of man – that was not within the range of their ideas; neither am I their enemy in all this, but it would be wrong in me to admit falsehood, or to stifle the truth.

Once more, then Theætetus, I repeat my old question, 'What is knowledge?' and do not say that you cannot tell; but quit yourself like a man, and by the help of God you will be able to tell.

– Plato, *Theætetus*

Notes

1. Plato, *Epistles*, R. G. Bury, tr, in Loeb Classical Library (London, New York, 1929), VII, 531
2. Withelm Windelbrand, *Präludien* (Freiburg and Tübingen, 1884), p9
3. Windelband, *Präludien*, pVI
4. Plato, *Apology*, H. N. Fowler, tr, in Loeb Classical Library (London, New York, 1913), I, p109
5. Karl Joel, *Geschichte der antiken Philosophie* (Tübigen, 1921), p770
6. Heinrich Maier, *Sokrates* (Tübingen, 1913), p157
7. Ulrich von Wilamowitz-Moellendorff, *Platon* (Berlin, 1919), I, p108
8. Immanuel Kant, *Critique of Pure Reason*, Norman Kemp Smith, tr (London, New York, 1933), p25
9. Kant, *Critique of Pure Reason*, pp31-32 (translation revised by Thomas K. Brown III)
10. J. F. Fries, *Die Geschichte der Philosophie* (Halle, 1837), I, p253
11. Plato, *Gorgias*, W. R. M. Lamb, tr, in Loeb Classical Library (London, New York, 1926), V, pp381-95
12. Plato, *Phaedrus*, H. N. Fowler, tr, in Loeb Classical Library (London, New York, 1913), I, p563
13. ibid., p565
14. Plato, *Epistles*, p537
15. ibid., pp531-3
16. Plato, *Epistles*, p541
17. Plato, *The Republic*, Paul Shorey, tr, in Loeb Classical Library (London, New York), p41
18. Kant, *Critique of Pure Reason*, p97
19. Plato, *Meno*, W. R. M. Lamb, tr, in Loeb Classical Library (London, New York, 1924), IV, p297.
20. ibid., pp299ff
21. Plato, *Meno*, p313
22. Kant, *Critique of Pure Reason*, p178
23. Plato, *Epistles*, pp527ff
24. Plato, *Epistles*, p539
25. J. F. Fries, *System der Logik* (3rd edn, re-issued, Leipzig, 1914), p449
26. Fries, *Die Geschichte der Philosophie*, I, p253
27. Fries, *System der Logik*, p436
28. ibid.
29. Maieutic: 'The word means performing midwife's services (to thought or ideas); Socrates figured himself as a midwife (maia) bringing others' thoughts to birth with his questionings...' (H. D. Fowler, *A Dictionary of Modern English Usage* [New York, 1944], p339.) See the quotation from Plato's Thætetus at the end of this essay.
30. George Berkeley, *The Analyst; or a Discourse Addressed to an Infidel Mathematician, Wherein it is Examined Whether the Object, Principles, and Inferences of the Modern Analysis are more Distinctly Conceived, or more Evidently Deduced, than Religious Mysteries and Points of Faith*. Selected Pamphlets, Vol. XVI (London, 1734).
31. Isaac Newton, *Philosophiae naturalis principia mathematica* (1687), Liber primus, scholium
32. Paul du Bois-Reymond, *Die allgemeine Funktionentheorie* (Tübingen, 1882), Pt I, p2
33. Karl Weierstrass, *Mathematische Werke* (Berlin, 1903), III, Appendix, pp315-29

Further information

Appendix 1
ORGANISATIONS OFFERING SOCRATIC ACTIVITIES

SFCP
Society for the Furtherance of the Critical Philosophy
SFCP, the sister educational charity of the PPA (see below), was established in Britain in 1940. During the Second World War it supported an experimental school, founded in Germany by the Kantian philosopher, Leonard Nelson, and his co-worker Minna Specht, which had taken refuge in Britain from the Nazis. Subsequently, other elements of the Society's objectives came into prominence and support was given to philosophical conferences, publications and a journal.

In recent years SFCP has sponsored:

- Scholarly research at doctoral and post-doctoral levels

- Socratic seminars for half days, full days and weekends for students in secondary schools, teachers of mathematics, education managers and other groups with varied backgrounds. With the introduction of citizenship into the UK school curriculum and the growing interest in philosophy, SFCP will be focusing more on acquainting teachers with the Socratic Method as a valuable tool for these subjects

- *The Occasional Working Papers in Ethics and Critical Philosophy* have attracted articles about Socratic Dialogue, including an English translation of Nelson's essay on the Socratic Method

Many of our activities involve networking to extend interest in Critical Philosophy and Socratic Dialogue among professionals across disciplines, and to encourage the fostering of ethical practice in everyday life.

- A two day residential Conference, *Ethics in Practice in the 21st Century*, convened in 1999; the published record of the Conference Proceedings laid the basis for further co-operation with a range of people and organisations
- Support in a variety of ways for academics in Bosnia

SFCP has a mailing list for those interested in its activities. A news bulletin is sent out once or twice a year and publications such as the *Occasional Working Papers* are listed and available on request.

SFCP – for further information contact:
Dr Rene Saran,
22 Kings Gardens,
London, NW6 4PU, UK
Tel.: 00 44 (0) 20 7328 1286
Fax: 00 44 (0) 20 7328 2552
Website: http://www.sfcp.org.uk

PPA
Philosophical-Political Academy
(Philosophisch-Politische Akademie)

PPA is dedicated to the promotion of Critical Philosophy, particularly as espoused by the German philosopher Leonard Nelson (1882-1927) and his followers, in its application to social and political life. In his writings, Nelson was concerned mainly with ethics, pedagogy and politics, and in all three fields he tried to put his theories into practice. He was an ethical socialist; he adapted Socrates' method of searching for truth, developing the neo-Socratic Method for group work. In 1922, he founded the PPA to further develop and promote his philosophical ideas. The PPA was banned by the Nazis but was re-established in 1949.

The Academy organises conferences on political and philosophical subjects; sponsors the publication of books; initiates scientific prize competitions; and, last but not least, supports Socratic seminars.

GSP
Society of Socratic Facilitators
(Gesellschaft für Sokratisches Philosophieren)

It is GSP's purpose to develop, in practice as well as in theory, Socratic Dialogue in the tradition of Nelson and Gustav Heckmann (1898 – 1996) who further developed Nelson's method; and to train facilitators. An increasing number of Socratic courses are organised by GSP, in co-operation with PPA, in different parts of Germany, and as interest in Socratic work has grown so has the need for more facilitators. During the 1980s and 1990s, courses were held three to five times a year, each recruiting up to forty people who work in small Socratic Dialogue groups of up to ten participants. Weekend seminars were introduced in response to demand.

Annual academic conferences related to the methodology of Socratic Dialogue have been added. *Sokratisches Philosophieren,* which is published annually, serves as a forum for discussion and also includes relevant papers. Beyond this, GSP contributes to the training of schoolteachers by acquainting them with Socratic Dialogue which will be valuable to those who are introducing the subject of practical philosophy in the curriculum of their schools.

PPA/GSP – for further information contact:
Dr. Dieter Krohn,
An den Papenstücken 21,
D 30455 Hannover, Germany
Tel: 00 49 (0) 511 49 69 14
Fax: 00 49 (0) 511 47 17 00
Website: http://www.philosophisch-politische-akademie.de

Dutch Network
of Socratic Facilitators

The Neo-Socratic Dialogue was introduced in the Netherlands around 1980; now there are about 25 Dutch facilitators. Most are united in a network, born out of the desire to exchange and learn from each other's experiences ('intervision') and so to improve their skills in facilitating Socratic Dialogues. Another purpose of the network is to promote the different forms of Socratic Dialogue, with different participants, but also in the context of business consultancy. In the network many aspects of the method of the Socratic Dialogue have been investigated; new 'arrangements' for Socratic Dialogue and training programmes for facilitators have been developed. This has been stimulated by the circumstances that all have the experience of the Socratic Dialogue in the context of business consultancy. Besides this, Socratic Dialogues are offered in secondary and higher education, and in adult education.

Several Dutch facilitators have facilitated Socratic Dialogues abroad, in English, German and French; have contributed to international conferences; and have trained Socratic facilitators abroad.

The network is not formalised in an association or society. The Dutch Society for Philosophical Practice (VFP), which has recently celebrated its 10th birthday, is currently preparing a proposal to start a sub-division dedicated to Socratic Dialogue. Once this has been established, the network will become part of this Society (VFP).

Dutch Network – for further information contact:
Dr Erik Boers
Akkerstraat 23
5615 HP Eindhoven
The Netherlands
Tel.: 00 31 40 29 61 985
Fax: 00 31 40 29 61 986
e-mail: virtus@wxs.nl

International co-operation
In Germany, for many years, participants from other countries, particularly the Netherlands, have taken part in Socratic seminars, with several becoming facilitators. In Britain, too, the Socratic Dialogue has aroused growing interest. In 1996 the first International Conference on the Critical Philosophy was convened at Hillcroft College, Surbiton, Surrey, organised by SFCP and supported by PPA. The second International Conference 'Socratic Dialogue: The Dutch Experience' was held in Leusden, Netherlands, in 1998, supported by PPA and SFCP. The third in this series was held in 2000 in Loccum, Germany, followed by the fourth in Birmingham, UK. Attendance has risen from 25 to 100 participants from twenty countries. Meanwhile, Socratic Dialogue has attracted interest in a number of other countries, including Japan, Australia, and Turkey and former communist countries in Eastern Europe.

Appendix 2

SOCRATIC DIALOGUE – PROCEDURES AND RULES

Procedures

The Socratic Dialogue normally uses the following procedures:

1. A well-formulated general question or a statement is set by the facilitator before the discourse commences

2. The first step is to collect examples experienced by participants which are relevant to the given topic

3. The group chooses one example, which will usually become the basis of the analysis and argumentation throughout the dialogue

4. Significant statements made by the participants are written down on a flipchart or board, so that all can have an overview of the discourse

Rules for participants

There are eight basic rules for participants in the Socratic Dialogue:

1. Each participant's contribution is based upon what s/he has experienced, not upon what s/he has read or heard

2. The thinking and questioning is honest. This means that only genuine doubts about what has been said should be expressed

3. It is the responsibility of all participants to express their thoughts as clearly and concisely as possible, so that everyone is able to build on the ideas contributed by others earlier in the dialogue

4. This means everyone listening carefully to all contributions. It also means active participation so that everyone's ideas are woven into the process of cooperative thinking

5. Participants should not concentrate exclusively on their own thoughts. They should make every effort to understand those of other participants and if necessary seek clarification

6. Anyone who has lost sight of the question or of the thread of the discussion should seek the help of others to clarify where the group stands

7. Abstract statements should be grounded in concrete experience in order to illuminate such statements. This is why a real-life example is needed and constant reference is made back to it during the dialogue

8. Inquiry into relevant questions continues as long as participants hold conflicting views or if they have not yet achieved clarity

Rules for facilitators
1. The main task of the facilitator is to assist the joint process of clarification so that any achieved consensus is genuine. Consensus is only achieved when contradictory points of view have been resolved and all arguments and counter-arguments have been fully considered; the facilitator has to ensure this happens

2. The facilitator should not steer the discussion in one particular direction nor take a position in matters of content

3. The facilitator should ensure that the rules of the dialogue are upheld, for instance watch that particular participants do not dominate or constantly interrupt the dialogue, whilst others remain silent

Criteria for suitable examples

1. The example has been derived from one's own particular experience; hypothetical or 'generalised' examples ('quite often it happens to me that...') are not suitable

2. Examples should not be very complicated; simple ones are often best. Where a sequence of events has been presented, it would be best for the group to concentrate on one event

3. The example has to be relevant for the topic of the dialogue and of interest to the other participants. Furthermore, all participants must be able to put themselves into the shoes of the person providing the example

4. The example should deal with an experience that has already come to an end. If the participant is still immersed in the experience it is not suitable. If decisions are still to be taken, there is a risk that group members might be judgemental or spin hypothetical thoughts

5. The participant giving the example has to be willing to present it fully and provide all the relevant factual information so that the other participants are able fully to understand the example and its relevance to the central question

Appendix 3

LITERATURE SURVEY ON SOCRATIC DIALOGUE

Fernando Leal

This is an attempt at a bibliographic essay on the Socratic Dialogue, which does not pretend to be exhaustive. The main purpose of it is to show that there is a budding literature on the practice of this form of dialogue in several countries. After referring to the original meaning of 'Socratic Dialogue' as a literary form, I proceed to the new meaning – not a literary form but an actual practice, which started some eighty years ago in Germany and has been cultivated ever since. I start with the founder of that practice, Leonard Nelson, and then survey the further developments of the method in the after-war period, as they are described in papers and books. The literature is not homogeneous, either in style or in the views expressed. Most of it is plainly written and unpedantic; and although some parts are more scholarly than others, there is a tendency not to stray too far from experience and practice. Not all people writing on the Socratic Dialogue agree on how best to use it or indeed on what it is. But such a state of affairs is more an asset than a liability if all Socratics are open-minded and ready to learn. I shall be glad if this modest attempt furthers that purpose.

The literary form of the Socratic Dialogue emerged in Athens around the time of Socrates' death. We know the names of a good dozen authors who wrote Socratic Dialogues, but apart from a handful of fragments we only possess those written by Xenophon and Plato. They both wrote a version of the speech given by Socrates (*Apology*) to defend himself against a charge of impiety, which include brief dialogues between him and his accusers. Both also wrote an account of a drinking party (*Symposium*) in which Socrates merrily engages in conversation with his friends. Xenophon wrote quite a long Socratic dialogue on the subject of estate management (*Oeconomicus*) and a collection of very brief dialogues on several moral issues (*Memorabilia*). Plato is the undisputed master of the genre, having written no less than seventeen short Socratic dialogues (*Euthyphro, Crito, Protagoras, Hippias Minor, Gorgias, Charmides, Ion, Laches, Meno, Lysis, Euthydemus, Phaedo, Phaedrus, Hippias Maior, Theatetus, Cratylus, Philebus*) and a very long one on the subject of politics (*The Republic*). The term 'Socratic Dialogue' refers in this context exclusively to a literary form in which the main character is called Socrates, having a more or less faithful relationship to the historical Socrates. Both Plato and Xenophon wrote other dialogues in which Socrates is not the main participant, although they are otherwise not essentially different from those already mentioned.

In this book the term 'Socratic Dialogue' has a different meaning. It refers not to fictional pieces in which someone *called* Socrates appears, but rather to real conversations among several people according to certain aims, rules, and procedures. A version of those rules appears in Appendix 2 of this book. The new meaning of 'Socratic Dialogue' was certainly inspired by some of Plato's Socratic dialogues, yet this does not mean that the fictional conversations contained in them follow those rules. In any case, a form of Socratic Dialogue which is recognisably related to the rules set forth in Appendix 2 was practised by Leonard Nelson (1882-1927), first in some of his seminars at Göttingen University, probably already during World War I, and certainly afterwards – and until his death in 1927 in the political groups he founded. An account of the method, and the first source of the new meaning of 'Socratic Dialogue' is a lecture he gave at the Göttingen Pedagogical Society in 1922, published in 1929. That paper, entitled 'The Socratic Method' was translated into English in 1949 (see chapter 13 of this book).

The tradition started by Leonard Nelson was cultivated by his friends, disciples, comrades, and followers after his death. One of them, Gustav Heckmann (1898-1996), was perhaps its most dedicated practitioner and the single most powerful factor in its further development and current widespread practice in Germany, the Netherlands and Britain. In particular, he is responsible for two important innovations to Nelson's method, *viz* the use of blackboard or flipchart to fix certain statements in writing, thus making them available to the whole group as shared property, and the device of a 'meta-dialogue', introduced to allow the group to discuss problems, both intellectual and emotional, which arise from the conduct of the dialogue. Heckmann's ideas and experiences with the Socratic Dialogue are described in his book, *Das sokratische Gespräch: Erfahrungen in philosophischen Hochschulseminaren* (Hannover, Hermann Schroedel Verlag, 1981; reprint in Frankfurt am Main, dipa-Verlag, 1993), of which some selections are translated into English as chapter 12 of the present volume. A short update of the book, centred on the meta-dialogue, is contained in the paper 'Über sokratisches Gespräch und sokratische Arbeitswochen', by Gustav Heckmann and Dieter Krohn (*Zeitschrift für Didaktik der Philosophie*, 1, 1988, pp38-43).

Several papers and books on the Socratic Dialogue have appeared in German since Heckmann's book. The *Festschrift* for Gustav Heckmann's 85th birthday (*Vernunft, Ethik, Politik*, edited by Detlef Horster and Dieter Krohn, Hannover, SOAK Verlag, 1983) contains papers by Hans Lehmann, Peter Kern and Hans-Georg Wittig, Fritz Eberhard, Wolfgang Klafki, Klaus-Rüdiger Wöhrmann, Detlef Horster, Otto-Friedrich von Hindenburg, Gisela Raupach-Strey, and Werner Kroebel. A paper by Detlef Horster ('Das sokratische Gespräch in der Erwachsenenbildung'), expounding some quite controversial ideas about the Socratic Dialogue, was published separately as volume 11 of the series *Theorie und Praxis* at Hannover University in 1986. (*See also* Horster's later work, *Das Sokratische Gespräch in Theorie und Praxis*, Opladen, Leske + Budrich, 1994.) A symposium on the Socratic Dialogue took place in 1988, and a book containing eight of the papers presented there was published (*Das sokratische Gespräch: ein Symposium*, edited by Dieter Krohn, Detlef Horster and Jürgen Heinen-Tenrich, Hamburg, Junius Verlag, 1989). A more recent attempt at bringing the Socratic Dialogue to the attention of the general public is the text selection *Das Sokratische Gespräch*, edited by Dieter Birnbacher and Dieter Krohn for the popular German series of the Reclam-Bändchen (Stuttgart, Reclam, 2002). It ranges from Plato's dialogue *Theaetetus* through Nelson's early essay to some important contemporary contributions.

In 1989 an informal in-house publication, the *Rundbrief der Sokratiker*, was launched to inform people about new ideas, developments, and topics of actual Socratic Dialogues. This was replaced in 1994 by a series called *Sokratisches Philosophieren*, which contains formal papers on both the Socratic Dialogue and more general philosophical topics. Of special interest for this survey are vols III (*Diskurstheorie und Sokratisches Gespräch*, 1996), IV (*Neuere Aspekte des Sokratischen Gesprächs*, 1997), VI (*Das Sokratische Gespräch: Möglichkeiten in philosophischer und pädagogischer Praxis*, 1999) and VII (*Das Sokratische Gespräch im Unterricht*, 2000). These were all published by dipa-Verlag (Frankfurt am Main). Forthcoming volumes, published by Lit Verlag (Münster) will contain, among other things, the proceedings of two international conferences on the Socratic Dialogue held in 2000 (Loccum, Germany) and 2002 (Birmingham, UK).

Some of the papers mentioned so far put forward interesting, although sometimes controversial proposals for the development of the Socratic Dialogue. They suggest its application to new problems or in new settings, and attempt a comparison of this method with other forms of dialogical communication discussed in the philosophical, pedagogical and psychological literature. In a similar vein, Rainer Loska's important monograph, *Lehren ohne Belehrung: Leonard Nelsons neosokratische Methode der Gesprächsführung* (Bad Heilbrunn, Verlag Julius Klinkhardt, 1995), is an extremely well-researched, meticulous and thoughtful study of the Socratic Dialogue as compared with other related methods for the teaching of mathematics at school level. Ute Siebert's *Das sokratische Gespräch: Darstellung seiner Geschichte und Entwicklung*, published in 1996, is a short history of the German tradition of the Socratic Dialogue, which purports to be the first instalment of a comparative study between the Socratic Dialogue and some African forms of discussion. Siebert's full study was recently completed and published as *Bildung vom Menschen aus: das Sokratische Gespräch im Entwicklungsprozess Einer Welt* (Kassel, Weber and Zucht, 2001). Finally, Gisela Raupach-Strey's *Sokratische Didaktik: die didaktische Bedeutung der Sokratischen Methode in der Tradition von Leonard Nelson und Gustav Heckmann* (Münster, Lit Verlag, 2002; included as volume X in the aforementioned series *Sokratisches Philosophieren*) is an encyclopaedic treatment of all questions pertaining to the use of the Socratic Dialogue in secondary education, especially for the teaching of philosophy and ethics.

Nelson used the Socratic Dialogue first in an educational setting but soon extended its application to the more clearly practical purposes of his own political organisations. In fact, he later changed the educational setting itself – from philosophical seminars at university level to his own special rural school, established for the education of children and also for the training of future political leaders. Nelson's followers continued these traditions both before and during World War II. A particularly striking example of the use of the Socratic Method within organised political activity refers to the question 'What is at stake in our fight against fascism? What are we defending here?', as facilitated by Nelson's disciple, Grete Henry-Hermann (1901-1984) with members of the German resistance movement (see Susanne Miller, *Occasional Working Papers in Ethics and the Critical Philosophy*, vol 2, 2000). Nelson's development of more practice-oriented Socratic Dialogue reaches back to the historical Socrates himself, who emphasised that his purpose was not just to examine people's beliefs but their lives. (*see* Pierre Hadot, *Philosophy as a way of life*, Oxford, Blackwell, 1995; and Michael Chase, *Occasional Working Papers in Ethics and the Critical Philosophy*, vol 2, 2000). Socrates was not interested in the question 'How ought we to live?' from a purely theoretical perspective; he wanted people to live better lives, more ethical lives; he was interested in action according to ethical values. And so was Nelson.

After World War II, the dissolution of Nelson's political organisation in Germany was causal in the restriction of the use of the Socratic Dialogue first to higher education and then to a kind of voluntary adult education, mostly in the form of residential courses over several days. The *spiritus rector* behind this work was Gustav Heckmann. However, some interesting changes have been occurring, especially since the 1990s, which mimic Nelson's own original development. On the one hand, a group of German educators, either trained by Heckmann himself or familiar with his work, have been experimenting with the Socratic Dialogue in more formal educational settings and in primary as well as secondary schools. On the other hand, a Dutch philosopher, Jos Kessels, originally trained in Germany among Heckmann's group of collaborators, has been pioneering the use of the Socratic Dialogue in different kinds of organisations – public and private, profit and non-profit, product-oriented and service-oriented – in the Netherlands. This controversial new development is described in his book, *Socrates op de markt: Filosofie in bedrijf* (Amsterdam, Boom, 1997; German translation as *Die Macht der Argumente: die sokratische Methode der Gesprächsführung in der Unternehmenspraxis*, Weinheim/ Basel, Beltz, 1997; English translation forthcoming), which refers the reader to some earlier papers (see also Dries Boele, The 'Benefits' of a Socratic Dialogue, Or: Which Results Can We Promise?, in *Inquiry: Critical Thinking Across the Disciplines*, XVII(3), Spring 1997, pp48-70). Both the German and the Dutch extensions (documented in volume IV of the series *Sokratisches Philosophieren*) constitute a beautiful example of the vitality of Nelson's tradition of Socratic Dialogue.

Nelson's lecture on the Socratic Dialogue has for many years served as a kind of introduction to the method for newcomers. Nevertheless, it is in the style of the 1920s. Contemporary readers may find it difficult to follow, so Rene Saran and I were commissioned to write a somewhat lighter version for our times. This we have done in the form of a fictional conversation between ourselves and an imaginary first-timer, called Anna. The first act (published in the *Occasional Working Papers in Ethics and the Critical Philosophy*, vol 2, 2002) takes place on the eve of Anna's first Socratic Dialogue and concerns itself with the doubts and queries of somebody who wants to participate but is somewhat daunted by the perspective of actually doing philosophy. The second act (to be published in the *Occasional Working Papers in Ethics and the Critical Philosophy*, vol 3, forthcoming) occurs at the end of Anna's first personal experience of the method and deals with the questions which arise in her mind as a result.

Finally, it can be argued that there is as yet no clear discussion of the place of the Socratic Dialogue within the tradition of Critical Philosophy that leads from Kant to Nelson and his followers. Nelson himself urged repeatedly that Critical Philosophy needs to be constantly renewed and further developed by each generation. The two tasks may belong together in such a way that one cannot tackle one whilst ignoring the other. A systematic attempt at clarification of the issues involved in relating the Socratic Dialogue to the critical tradition is the main aim of a series of papers I have written. These appeared in the *Occasional Working Papers in Ethics and the Critical Philosophy* (see The Future of the Critical Philosophy and What is the Link between the Critical Philosophy and the Socratic Dialogue in vol 1, as well as The Relation between Value Conflicts and the Socratic Dialogue in vol 2). More recently, I have also tried to bring the Socratic Dialogue in contact with recent research in the multidisciplinary field of implicit theories and mental models, in my paper: El diálogo socrático como método de investigación de teorías implícitas (see E. Matute and R.M. Romo-Beltrán, eds, *Los retos de la educación del siglo XXI*, Universidad de Guadalajara, Mexico, 2001).

I wish to dedicate this modest bibliographic essay to the memory of Nora Walter (1923-2001). Like Socrates, Nora didn't write papers, monographs, or treatises. Yet she showed us through her life what it means to be Socratic.

Appendix 4

ORIGINAL SOURCES

The editors are grateful for permission to reproduce texts from the following original sources:

PART I

Chapter 2   Birnbacher, Dieter and Krohn, Dieter, eds (2002) *Das sokratische Gespräch*, Stuttgart: Phillip Reclam jun, pp7-13

Chapter 3   Krohn, Dieter (1998) Theorie und Praxis des Sokratischen Gesprächs, in Lohmann, Karl Reinhard and Schmidt, Thomas, eds, *Akademische Philosophie zwischen Anspruch und Erwartung*, Frankfurt am Main: Suhrkamp, pp119-132

PART II

Chapter 4   Imison, Tamsyn (2002) A Personal View of Education, Schools as Learning Communities, *Newsletter of Philosophy of Education Society of Great Britain*, pp33-34

Chapter 5   Saran, Rene and Neisser, Barbara (2000) How can Socratic Dialogue be used in Ethics Lessons in School? Workshop Paper at Third International Conference on *Socratic Dialogue and Ethics*, Loccum, Germany, July (to be published in conference proceedings)

Chapter 6   Delgehausen, Ingrid (2000) Erfahrungen mit dem Sokratischen Gespräch im Grundschulunterricht, in Krohn, Dieter, Neisser, Barbara and Walter, Nora eds, Das Sokratische Gespräch im Unterricht,

	Sokratisches Philosophieren, Frankfurt am Main: dipa-Verlag, VII, pp55-60
Chapter 7	Saran, Rene (1998) Socratic Dialogue in a secondary school, *Management in Education*, 12(3), pp8-10
Chapter 9	Goldstein, Mechthild (2000) Wir mussten selber denken. Ein Sokratisches Experiment im Mathematikunterricht der Jargangsstufe 8 und 9 einer Hauptschule, in Krohn, Dieter, Neisser, Barbara and Walter, Nora eds, Das Sokratische Gespräch im Unterricht, *Sokratisches Philosophieren*, Frankfurt am Main: dipa-Verlag, VII, pp48-54
Chapter 10	Neisser, Barbara (1997) Das Sokratische Gespräch im Philosophieunterricht in Krohn, Dieter, Neisser, Barbara and Walter, Nora eds, Neuere Aspekte des Sokratischen Gesprächs, *Sokratisches Philosophieren*, Frankfurt am Main: dipa-Verlag, IV, pp88-102

PART III

Chapter 11	Raupach-Strey, Gisela (2002) *Sokratische Didaktik. Die didaktische Bedeutung der Sokratischen Methode in der Tradition von Leonard Nelson und Gustav Heckmann*, chapter V.1, sections on 'Das positive Potential des Sokratischen Paradigmas am Lernort Schule: vier Modelle', 'Das Sokratische Paradigma im Kontext der Fächer' and 'Dialogische Deutung der Unterrichtssituation', Münster – Hamburg – London: LIT-Verlag, pp374-385 and 386-387
Chapter 12	Heckmann, Gustav (1981) *Das sokratische Gespräch. Erfahrungen in philosophischen Hochschulseminaren*, Hannover: Hermann Schroedel Verlag, pp66-71 and pp79-82
Chapter 13	Nelson, Leonard (1998) The Socratic Method, with an Introduction by Leal, Fernando, in *Occasional Working Papers in Ethics and the Critical Philosophy*, London: SFCP, 1, April, pp42-62
	Nelson's essay on Die Sokratische Methode dates back to 1922, and was first published in English in Nelson, Leonard (1949) *Socratic Method and Critical Philosophy: Selected Essays*, New Haven: Yale University Press and republished by Dover Publications in 1965

Printed in the United Kingdom
by Lightning Source UK Ltd.
109691UKS00001BA/1-60